SONG OF THE MONK

ROHIT DEY

Contents

Preface

Before scribbling my thoughts into words on these white pages, let me share a simple story about the self 'I Am'. It wasn't very long when I would wake up with thousands of thoughts bulging up in my mind, like-I have to work harder, I have to outperform others to get success, promotions, name and fame in this world, and I had to be better than the rest because I believed that there was a race out there and I had to defeat all!

When I would wake up, my mind would continuously wonder around such thoughts. It kept on scaring me of the coming days, and the efforts that were required in order to make my future more prominent and better, wouldn't allow me to stay in the present moment and enjoy it. My anxiety and ambition drove me back and forth to strive for perfection, perfection by not just improving oneself but perusing others to be imperfect, and it made me irritable, even angry at myself when I couldn't do so. I had heard that striving for perfection is the way to progress, but what was required to achieve it was turning me into an uncompassionate and unempathetic human being. It wasn't that I was not doing as a professional, but I had started to realise that I was intimidated by the growth of my yearning for more and more.

Deep down inside, this made me very unhappy! And I chose to seek a solution; I did almost whatever it needed. I followed the distractions-took holidays, picked up new hobbies which led me nowhere, found new escapes in unknown places, indulged in movies and theatre, bought a new cell phone which claimed to be smarter than I am, took advice from a few close friends, and even went to a psychologist. But nothing worked for me, not even a little bit.

One day, almost in frustration, I decided to take a day off from work. And I decided to do nothing! I laced my shoes tight and went to a nearby park for a leisurely walk. It was a regular park with a big fountain in the middle, dense trees, and pruned shrubs around the garden. There were lots of birds chirping with their fellow mates quite loudly. And there were plenty of people-all walking and engrossed. Suddenly, it started raining, and everyone started running for shelter to hide their heads under the shade. People seemed more worried about their smartphones since they were drenched in the rain, and their currency notes should not get wet in this heavy rainfall. Indeed! It should not??

Amidst all this, there was a little girl. With one hand, she was holding her mother, and with the other she was gathering the fresh raindrops falling on her tiny palm, looking up in the sky and tasting the droplets with a smile. She was continuously doing that, besides being chided by her mother many times; she was still catching the raindrops with her little hand and was absorbed in absolute delight and happiness. The only thing that I learned from this incident is that, among all of us, she was the only one who was continuously happy! Why was she so blissful and the rest of us were reluctantly miserable all the time? I got my answer. It's because, among all of us standing there, she was the only person who was one with nature; with her palm facing up towards the sky, whereas ours were down, mostly in our pockets, preserving the riches.

On this planet which is billions of years old, with billions of people around, why I as an individual was trying to outshine everyone that lives or has lived on this planet? What was I trying to do, just fooling myself? That thought humbled me down for good. That day taught me a profound lesson. I was calm, kind, considerate, and relatively happy throughout the day. Because of that innocent child, I had learned the biggest lesson of my life: Why to be happy when there is nothing to be lament about? I asked myself a series of questions to know what I wanted and how much I was willing to give up or sacrifice in order to achieve that. While doing that as honestly as I could, I understood the truth of the 'Am-ness' in me and the 'I-ness' in all. And once I chose to be conscious and aware of my being, my mind started becoming calm and contained. Perhaps many of us – teachers, doctors, lawyers, people in business, artists, and other professionals – are dealing with or have often dealt with a similar dilemma during a lifetime.

While seeking an answer to all these questions, I made a clear choice to try and find it for all. If you ask these questions to yourself, you will probably start figuring out what are you or more preciously, who you are. But whatever be the path you may freely choose to seek your answers from, could be different from mine and that is okay since this difference of choices is what defines us – who or what we really are! The ancient literature and the literary heritage of our country: the profound teachings of our greatest spiritual masters and their effulgent transcriptions, commentaries on the Vedas, Upanishads, Puranas, Gita's etc have been inspiring millions of us, time and again and it will continue to do so.

It is believed that 'we are all spiritual beings having a temporary human experience'. We keep coming back to this planet again and again as long as we don't realise the true nature and the true divinity of our 'being-ness' or the blissfulness of being conscious about the existence – 'Sat-Chit-Ananda'.

The ignorance of this fundamental principal of 'Sat-Chit-Ananda' leads us to the disconnection between the unreal and the real, the untruth and the truth, the darkness and the light, which becomes the bedrock of all human miseries and sufferings. This principle reality of human existence is more clearly articulated in the great scriptures like in the Vedas and the Upanishads, in the highest teaching of the Gita, in the supreme verses of the Vedanta, in the sublime commentaries of the Brahma-sutra, also in the morality lessons of the Ramayana and Mahabharata. When I was first introduced to the stories of the Ramayana and the Mahabharata at a very young age by my grandparents as folklore, I was left perplexed, holding numerous questions in my heart that could barely be answered most of the time. Why did Rama have to kill Ravena if killing is what I was taught to be a sinful act or an act of crime? Why do good people always cry while bad people enjoy all the perks?

But I am grateful that my tender mind was not sown with any biassed answers or interpretations by them... rather the truth prevailed to be untold and it is me who was driven to find them once

I grow up wise, if at all someday? This seed of deep inquiry within me has become the joy of my life and made me the person solely responsible for finding my own truth.Over the years, I committed myself to discovering all the possibilities of studying and understanding the truth about human life from various interpreters, great gurus, religious scriptures, lengthy commentaries, and translations, to understand what is that one thing that holds and integrates everything to be one, or what is that one ultimate reality which is manifested in many but remains veiled from the frame of my awareness.

The "Song of the Monk" is a modest attempt to convey and share my limited understanding of "Human Existence" in order to know the truth of the "I" in me and the "You" in all of us. It brings to light many of the questions that most of us often shy away from and are more comfortable if they are left unanswered. This book is an endeavour where you, who dare to, and I, shall try to know over the due course of time, in the form of various questions seeking an answer or the right path to stay on until the realisation happens and the reality of "WHO AM I" is known, shining within us maybe in this life or many, many lives after.

To explore this enduring fascination for my questions being answered in the right direction, I am on a journey as I have been trying to read and understand the essence of spiritual knowledge through religious scriptures that are widely available to us in the form of books, commentaries and lectures. Texts like the Ramayana, the Mahabharata, the Gita and many other such inspired scriptures of the Indic civilisation seem to provide all the possible answers that are hidden only within us about the "Supreme Existence". They also try to throw light on the concept of right and wrong, or if anything is called right or wrong at all.

I am glad, indeed, to be able to put forward a few words of my understanding, and the purpose of this writing is just a humble effort to ponder over this one question again, about realising the real meaning of human life and recognising the reality of our own existence in the vastness of self-effulgent light.

~ Rohit

ACKNOWLEDGEMENTS

This book has been an intensive journey of confusion, conflict, churning, and synthesis as I wove my interpretations of old Indian knowledge into a coherent discourse. Therefore, I would want to convey my thanks to Swami sarvapriyananda Ji Maharaj (English Lectures) Swami Samarpanananda Ji Maharaj (Bengali lectures), whom I consider my mentors and whose works and lectures motivated me to undertake this project. I am also grateful to my family and friends for supporting me in my endeavour.

LET'S DIVE IN!

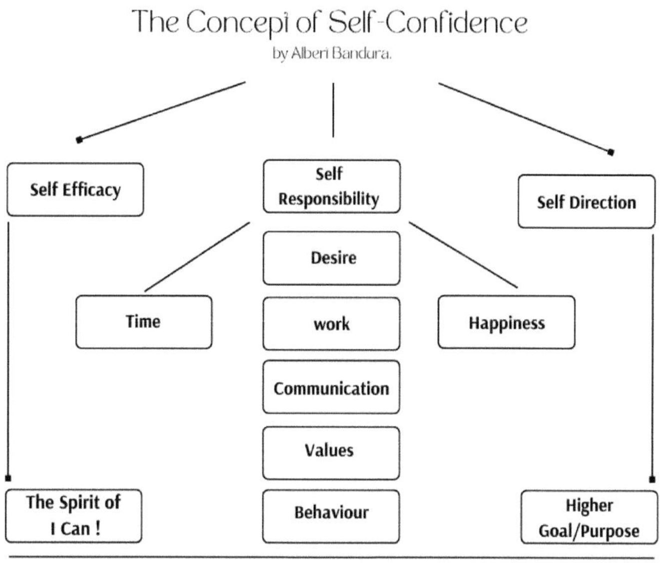

The Concepi of Self-Confidence

by Alberi Bandura.

Self Efficacy

Self Responsibility

Self Direction

Desire

Time

work

Happiness

Communication

Values

The Spirit of I Can !

Behaviour

Higher Goal/Purpose

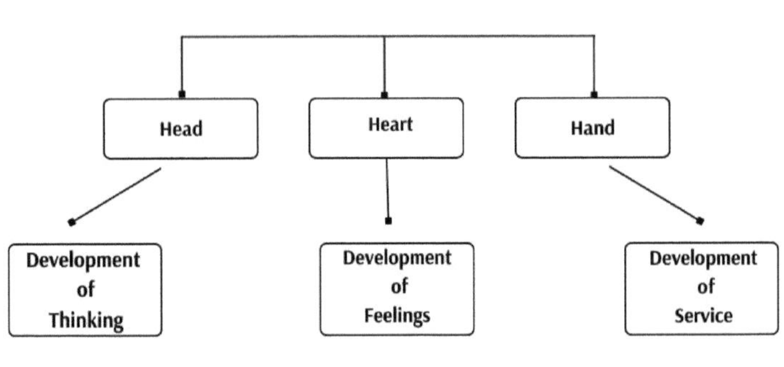

START WITH THE SMALLEST ; PRACTICE THE EASIEST

~ ***SWAMI SARVAPRIYANANDA***

The Technique of SQRRR

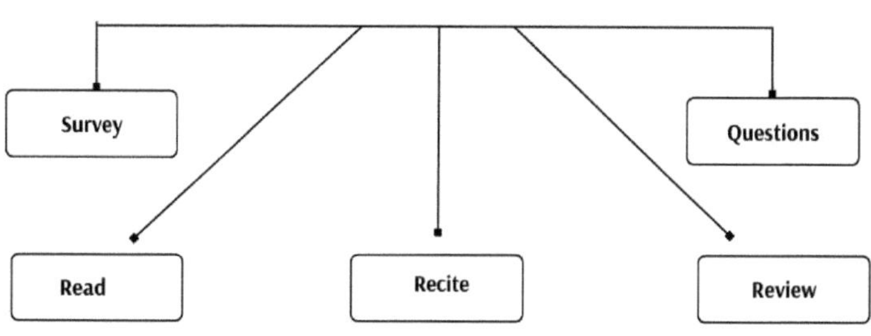

"Do whatever you are doing with the fullest possible attention. This is the essence of concentration."

~ Swami Vivekananda

CHANTING

"

ॐ असतोमा सद्गमय । तमसोमा ज्योतिर् गमय । मृत्योर्मामृतं गमय ॥ ॐ शान्ति शान्ति शान्तिः ।।

AUM...asato mā sadgamaya | tamasomā jyotir gamaya || mrityormāamritam gamaya |AUM...shānti shānti shāntiḥ: ||

'AUM'...lead me from unreal to the real | lead me from darkness to light || lead me from death to immortality |'AUM'...peace, peace, peace: ||

"

AVOWAL

"...if you single-mindedly chase pleasure, very soon, you find nothing pleasing anymore."

~ Somerset Maugham in the 'Razor's Edge.

Seeing The Infinity Within!

"When the nectar of life flows-
Pouring on from one to the another,
Then arises the need for love and sanctity, joy and sagacity
But where on earth such things can you trace...?
Which is abounding of all divine grace.
When the dark hours thrust you into abyssal depths,
From where does emerge the eternal light..?
Turn inward, deep within...
Maybe then you find an inner spark
Effervescent enough to enkindle the universe... and I?
So says the Monk, let the light of the day be yours.
And I shall burn like a flame in the night.
Let the flowers in your garden be all roses.
And I shall shield it as thorns from sunless to sunlight.
Let the food be all yours, of pleasure and pride;
And I shall drink the pain of a mother-
Giving birth to a new life.
Let the things in the world be all yours.
And I shall hold on to nothing to fight.
Let that victorious smile be always yours.
And I shall curtail your defeats into a delight.
Let the realm of intelligence be always yours...
And I shall spread the wisdom of compassion and love.
Thus to know,
The infinite almighty (Nirguna) is reborn into humanity (Saguna) as the "Us"!
Where the mortals drink the nectar to procure immorality, as nectar so does... (Moksha)
~ an invocation to the eternel infinity [Brahman]"

The Way Of Action

I

Imagination

"...what is good and what is bad; who shall decide, what should be the fate? Where the one gets many, many gets, not even a penny! Is there more to living a dream than just dreaming for a greater life?"

Dhruv is a normal teenage boy who belongs to a lower-middle-class family. His father works on farmland, and his mother looks after the home and manages the things inside. Dhruv has developed a strong interest in cricket. In fact, he wants to be a famous cricketer like Sachin Tendulkar. He spends most of his time playing cricket and very little time in school or studying. But he is the topper of most boys in his entire class. Being the village boys, they initiated everything and copied their essential needs in their own style. They shaped a log of wood to look like a wooden bet; for wickets behind, they arranged some nice bamboo trees, chopped them from the bottom, and got stumps to dig in the sand. They used to go to some aristocratic families and work in their houses just to make some money and buy a cricket ball. That is how they arrange all the tools needed to play the game of cricket. They had a great time playing their game and even drew a small crowd for them. The group of elderly people who live in their village do nothing but play cards with their neighbours under the shade of a banyan tree. So this jobless old crowd becomes the spectators for the young cricketer's group. They even cheer them up and enjoy the game more than they play on their own.

Among them, all one of Dhruv's friends, Kumar, used to have a rejected piece of mic that his father brought him from the electronic store he worked in, and with that very piece of mic, Kumar tried to do the part of commentary, but unfortunately, the mic produced no louder sound than the range of his poor voice. And with that, Dhruv and the troops had all their essential tools and requirements to play a cricket game. Dhruv goes to his home after the game gets over. But the game gets over only when all the poor kids feel their stomachs empty, as they haven't eaten anything since the morning. So all the boys rushed to their mother's for food. Like all the other mothers do, first they beat them hard-handed, then they feed them a full meal too. The emotion of a mother for her child is just an unconditional feeling of love. Dhruv asked his mom for food, and she gave him the food, but not before she regulated his ears from the north to the south. Dhruv's mother likes the game of cricket very much, and yet she hates this game the most. In her childhood days, she used to play with her brother Prakash. Prakash wants to be a cricketer like Dhruv. But he was born into a poor family, and his father could not afford to give him 2000 bucks to participate in the post-state level selection match. He could not say anything to his father as he was well aware of his humble family background and belonged to, but then he could not bear the undeniable poverty of life as it is. He hanged himself from a ceiling fan, and he died. And that is why Dhruv's mother does not want to see one more death in his family because of the same game of cricket. So she warned Dhruv not to play this game but to study hard and get a good job. But Dhruv is very much a prominent cricketer despite anything. He kept on playing cricket in the same fashion, and over the next few days, he transformed into a very good cricketer in his village. He can make a score as fast as anything, and by the end of his schooling, he will have a lot of meddles and trophies. He passed out of schooling and he scored an outstandingly good result of 80% in all the subjects. And now he is all set to go to the next level.

The first year of college life starts well for Dhruv. For the first time, he has met students outside of his circle and from many other different places, many boys and girls in unison. He, too, was excited, and at the same time, he was a bit nervous as well. Because he has scored a good result in his last exams, he has been both awarded and rewarded with money and study materials, and that's how he earns for his own future. The local government announced that his studies are free for the next two years and that they will also provide the books and study materials. Dhruv made his parents feel proud of him and also helped them out of a lot of expenses incurred in his studies. But Dhruv was meant to be a cricketer, and he was living the same dream.

Every year, the college's annual sports days begin. Students are getting themselves ready for various games and to participate in them to win the title, of course. So, because Dhruv is also a member of his college sports team, he was assigned to the position of 12th man on the team. And if anyone from the top 11 gets injured during the game, then only he may get a chance to play for his team, or else it is only in the hands of team captain Ajay. Ajay belongs to a very rich family and his father acts as a trusty for that very college. And that is one of the reasons that Ajay has been chosen as the team captain. So, the sport starts as usual on a normal day. It was the first match between South Point Public College and Summer-Salt National College. Dhruv didn't get a chance to play. He remained there as the 12th person who usually used to bring drinks for the rest of the players during breaks. Yet Dhruv was so passionate about cricket that he never even did that either. He is a true lover of his cricket passion more than anything or any position.

It was the 13th over of the match when one of his teammates suddenly got injured. Quick delivery from the opposition hits him hard and he falls down to the ground, and hence he has to leave the ground for medicals. Moreover, he was the lead bowler for their team as well. So, having no option left for the team captain, Ajay, he has to include Dhruv in the team. Dhruv batted brilliantly for his team, allowing them to defeat the opposing team by a large margin. Dhruv scored a good 40 runs for his team and managed to get 3 wickets. But Ajay was chosen for the man of the match award. He scored 50 runs in 90 balls. Dhruv didn't even mind that at all. He is a genuine cricket player who doesn't play to get awards, he plays for his team to win matches.

Raju is the funniest boy in Dhruv's class. He is so poor in his studies that most of the time the teachers like to keep him out of the class rather than in it. He throws jokes and acts funny to entertain his fellow college mates. But he is a big-hearted fellow in the entire class, as Dhruv has remarked. Dhruv and Raju became good friends over time, and their friendship starts with a funny scene.

One day, when Dhruv was sitting in his class, all of a sudden, Raju turned up before him, and he started asking him for 10 bucks. Dhruv had 30 bucks in his pocket, so he gave him the same. A few minutes later, he turned up again and started asking for another 10 rupees, which Dhruv gave him. But a minute later, Raju turned up again to ask for another 10 rupee note from Dhruv. Dhruv became irritated with Raju's behaviour and refused to give him the change. Dhruv has just got 10 bucks left for his bus fare home. But then Dhruv changed his mind and decided to give him the last few bucks as well. That's all he had left in his hand. He thinks that maybe Raju wants it for some great reason. He asked Raju and told him that he wouldn't have any money left in his pocket and that he had already given him all 30 bucks. So he wants to know why he is asking for more money. Raju nodded his head down and upheld his hand, taking him out of the class. They reached a place where a woman was begging for food for her two children, yet she was due for a third birth. Her husband left her alone in this situation. Raju promised the lady to give 10 bucks to each of her sons, but when he put his hands in his pockets, he got nothing more than the remaining cotton and dust particles. But he promised her he would give her the money, so he chose to get it from some of his close friends. Apparently, everyone had refused to give him the money, but when he asked the same to Dhruv, he gave it to him without any refusal or even asking Raju any question to know the reason why. As a result, they became good friends for life.

It was the final year of college for Dhruv. And by the time Raju and Dhruv became best friends, a friendship with Dhruv helped Raju get a meritorious lift into the lists of good students. Now Raju too gets his place inside the class and not outside, so even the teachers praise him for his studious transformation.

One day, Dhruv asked Raju to take him to his home. Raju had never spoken to Dhruv about his family or parents, even though they had known each other for a long time. Raju looked to be a very happy person all the time; he smiled just like a great sage does, hiding behind the deep emotions that cry inside his heart and showing the world a smiley face every time. Dhruv was able to study the lines written in big bold letters on a board when they arrived at Raju's place because Raju didn't say anything and took him straight to the place where he lives with all of his family members—Holy Children Orphan House.

Raju has no parents. In fact, he doesn't even know who gave him birth or who his parents are. Mom and Dad? As rightly said by the Sister of the Orphan House, the only thing that he knows about them is that they are not alive in this world. Dhruv feels sad for Raju, and he hugs him one more time. Raju smiled while his tears rolled down from his fragile eyes. And he utters these words to Dhruv: "The only reason you are crying, Dhruv, is because you feel pity for me because I don't have a family; but I am crying now because at least I have got a brother in you who I think is my family too."

Dhruv is shining everywhere in the class. He has become the igniting mind among all the understudies in the class. His teachers like him because he is humble and simple, and he is also a good student. Ajay, being the richest of the leads in the student crowd, sensed jealousy about Dhruv's priority, even though his jealousy was turned off by the grandeur of respect and friendship shown by Dhruv through his plight of behaviourism. Dhruv knows the truth that only love can beat the blackness of cruel hearts... and hatred couldn't. So a friend, like a believer, always gulfs the gap between him and the others, anyone who comes towards his aura, and so it happened with Ajay as well. At the same time, he too becomes good friends with Dhruv.

The second year of annual sports dates were announced, and Ajay this time requested Dhruv to be the team captain and lead his team. He wants to play under him as a team unit and not as the rich kid. Dhruv obliged the post by taking the captaincy with more conviction and responsibility. He led the team forward to host the first match against the opposition, i.e S.P.P.C vs S.S.N.C once again.

The S.P.P. college cricket team is captained by Dhruv. The match starts and both teams' players meet on the ground. The partnership between Ajay and Dhruv took the team score to 165-0 in 10 overs. Ajay scored a well-deserved 55 runs and Dhruv played a brilliant innings of 102 runs without losing any wickets. And both of them hug each other, appropriate each other, and leave the ground after their innings are over. Like this, the next innings start in fashion. Dhruv executed his field tactics well and he placed his players in the right positions. By the end of eight overs against the opponent, the team could only score 70, losing four of the crucial wickets. Dhruv's accurate captaincy makes it difficult for the S.S.N.C team to score in the full swim. Even their remaining wickets were falling down so often that it was hard for them to keep them together.

But then, something worse happens to the S.P.P.C team. Dhruv's teammate and best friend collapsed to the ground in the ninth over of the match and has since lost consciousness. The game had been called off, and all the mates rushed towards Raju, and soon, with the help of the college authorities, they took Raju to the hospital. The doctors have reportedly said that Raju has a hole in his heart and it has grown worse over time due to ignorance or negligence. There should have been an early treatment for its cure, but now it seems too flexible to take any measures to save Raju's life. Raju had a paralytic attack, and maybe he won't live too long if he isn't operated on now. Dhruv overheard the talk, and he asked the doctor not to speak badly about his friend. He rushed to see Raju, surviving the pain of death. Some days later, one of the senior sports association members, Mr. Surrender Singh, called Dhruv in his office and informed him that he had been shortlisted for the Inter-State Team Matches because of his good skills. A glow of happiness rays down on Dhruv's face after he hears about his dream selection. He folds his hands in front of the person and greets him warmly. But at the end of his speech to Dhruv, the gentleman asked him to pay a token amount of Rs 50,000 for his selection fee. The news makes him appear even sadder than he was previously. He left the hall and went straight to his home

After reaching home, he sat down in some lonely corner of his room and began to lament his poor condition. But he also knew that he or his poor parents couldn't even afford the demand... and so his dream of playing for the country remained a dream. While he was crying all alone, his mother heard the emotional puffs coming out of the next room. She enters his room and approaches him to find out what has just happened. Dhruv wants to hide the truth from his mother, but like every mother, she can also easily catch hold of his son's grief in friction. Dhruv then had to tell his mother about everything good and bad, and after listening to his son's voice, she too broke into tears. It was the same kind of situation that she had experienced before with her own brother, Prakash, as well. His history is repeating itself back to his family once again, yet the situation remains the same in poverty. She could now experience her brother's face within Dhruv himself. She rushed to somewhere, unlocked the savings, and got some gold ornaments out of one old box. She gave it to Dhruv to go sell them all and see if he could pay the amount, at least because she had already seen a dream die before her own naked eyes, her own brother's, and now she could not allow the situation to take the passion of his child dying. She gave him the box and ordered him to make appropriate use of these meaningless goods for the best of his life and career. Dhruv hugs his mother, and they both shade their treas together.

The next morning, Dhruv arranged the required amount of money in his hand to give it to the team selector. So he was very happy and excited to see his dream come true. He decided to meet his friend Raju before he went and give the full amount to the selector's hand, and also to tell Raju about his joy. So he went to the hospital to meet his friend Raju, lying on his bed lifelessly. But there he got one more blow in the light of his existence. The doctors rushed to Dhruv and asked to clear him of the balance and also to take his friend out of the hospital. For them, Raju is one such impossible case, and they couldn't do anything to save him, or maybe they just don't want to operate anyone for free to save lives. He is just taking a bed and wasting it completely. The doctor then gave Dhruv a list of bills and asked him to pay immediately and take his friend out of the centre. And when he saw the bill of Rs. 50000/-Dhruv was driven off by the pathetic conditional situation of life once again. One way is to lead him to ultimate success, and the other is to ask for help from humanity, i.e., to save his friend's life. But Dhruv was very profound and proudly chose the flag of friendship to raise the mere dream of success.

Dhruv deposited his entire money at the hospital and took his friend Raju to his home after they signed the discharge. His mother feels proud to have given birth to Dhruv, and that she has genuinely offered this world the real star from her womb... Dhruv.

Dhruv then never fulfilled his dream of being a cricketer and playing games for his nation, but he struggled hard to change his world and became a great cricket coach. He then starts his own sports academy for young cricketers who have the passion to play the game of cricket.

II

Action in Inaction, Inaction in Action

There are several meditation schools, each with their own set of procedures, methods, and practises. If these practises are followed on a daily basis, a person may achieve a certain degree of enlightenment. They may become aware of, or experience, an amazing condition known as "Awakening!" This whole philosophy and practise is nothing more than mechanical repetition, and it is not really meditation. Is it feasible, however, to put a stop to this never-ending mental chatter? Is it possible to meditate and be completely aware of the flow of your thoughts without trying to stop them or control them, and to be aware of "awareness" alone?

Thought can only exist in the form of words or images. Meditation does not include fantasising or being absorbed in some fanciful insight. Meditation, as opposed to a suppression-or conformity-based discipline, demands remarkable self-control. Self-discipline emerges as a result of thinking monitoring. Discipline is achieved through observing the chain of one's own thoughts. Thought observation leads to a thorough awareness of the mind and its subtle discipline, which is essential for meditation. There is no time restriction for meditation. It is feasible to do it at any time;

it is even possible to do it while travelling on a bus. True meditation is being completely aware of what is going on in and around oneself, as well as what is going on inside oneself, and being cognizant of the whole situation. Meditation is a way to clear your mind of all the things that distract you so you can feel the million sparks of a single breath.

In the absence of knowledge, the known is left unrealised, and the unknown has no meaning in the calmness of the mind. To see anything new, the mind must be empty of all the past. Truth or God or whatever name is given to that one-alone reality must be unique and not something that is the result of propaganda, which is the result of conditioning... So, God or truth should not be the result of an outcome. The truth is, something lives every day. Therefore, the mind must be empty to see the truth. And this emptying of the mind without any prerequisite thought is meditation to realise "What is..." rather than the "How or Why?" "What is" is not a static thing, but it is a thing that is alive and now. So, a meditative mind is said to be a silent mind without any thoughts or actions. Silence is not the product of the suppression of noise, or the opposite of noise. It comes only when the mind has wholly known and understood itself. Hence, there are no movements at all in mind. In that silence, everything happens; everything is known; everything is being observed at once. That is actual meditation, not a phoney acceptance of authority and repetition of words.

Karma is compressed into its three essential elements: the individual, the acts of the individual, and the results of those individual acts. All of this put together in one chain of action is called "Karma". Now, one may ask, what is the law of karma then? Karma, or action, has its consequences. Good actions result in merit, and merit results in happiness. In contrast, nasty actions, which we might consider evil when consciously done, result in a demerit, and the result of lousy actions leads to unhappiness. In other words, when the sense of doer-ship is attached to its doings, it gives birth to "I," the doer who feels "I did the doing." If I do something nice, it feels good, and if I do something nasty, I feel guilty for his/her action. "I," the doer, owns the outcome of the action and thus appears to receive the outcomes as well.This is the "Law of Karma."

Hinduism, Buddhism, Jainism, Sikhism, and other Indian religions are explicitly based on the "Law of Karma". Despite their vast internal diversities and differences, they all accepted the "law of karma" as being real and happening. [Buddhism does not accept God (the permanent unchanging self-'Ishwara'), but it agrees with the law of karma.] However, Advaita Vedanta (Non-dual Philosophy) contradicts the "LoK" as being unreal, hence it doesn't exist. Advaita Vedanta divides reality into three tiers: absolute, transactional, and illusion.

The waker in the waking state experiences a transactional reality (seeing, hearing, smelling, tasting, touching). In his dreamy vision, the dreamer experiences the illusions of the mind (happiness and anxiety). In the deep sleep state, the experiencer experiences a deep dark 'nothingness'. But the ultimate knower of all three forms of reality is the absolute truth (God/Brahman/Atman/Turiyam). So, what Vedanta is trying to do is to shift us from identification with the entities of empirical reality to absolute truth. [Mandukya Upanishad]

Say, for example, you were reading this book in your dream, and somebody in the dream comes and tells you that whatever you are doing (reading a book) is inhabited by a dream, but the reality is that you are sleeping on your bed imagining all this. Take note that the bed on which you are sleeping and imagining a dream is not a part of the dream, and if you go around in the dream looking for the bed on which you are sleeping and imagining, you will never find it because the reality is that you are sleeping on your bed and imagining an illusion created by your mind. And that is the truth. Similarly, this entire world of appearances is grounded in absolute reality.

What is good and what is evil? Who can decide what should be their fate? In "The Song of the Sannyasin," which is a song by Swami Vivekananda, he says it well:

"... good, good; bad, bad. And none.

Escape the law, but who so wears a form
Must bear the chain. " Too true. But far beyond
Both name and form is Atman, ever free.
Know thou art That, Sannyasin bold! Say,
"Om tat sat, Om!"

Therefore, whatever work we may do in our life, good or bad, must reflect upon the self: who is doing it and what he is doing at the end. If he does a good deed, the reward must be according to that; or if he does something terrible, no matter the reason, he will have to accept the consequences that no one can escape. Whoever is identified with the body and mind is also identified with a load of their past deeds and misdeeds. Far beyond, like the waking transcends the dream, the absolute transcends the relative and remains only in the absoluteness, knowing "thou art that". The oasis and a real desert can coexist, as can an unreal snake and a real rope. However, you can't sleep or dream unless you're awake; a false mirage can't appear unless there's a real desert; and a false snake can't appear unless there's a real rope.Just that, the real rope, the desert, or the state of wakefulness [This] are all based on a higher level of reality, which is referred to as‘ pure consciousness' [That]. So, 'this' cannot affect 'that' but that gives 'this' existence and 'that' thing which gives 'this' existence. That is what you and I really are.

"Not one grain of sand in the desert can be made wet by the water of the mirage," says Adi Shankaracharya. By this faith, the law of karma will continue to appear to function and to give results. Still, it doesn't affect you, and that part of you that isn't affected is called "Atman." Atman is the absolute you that isn't affected by the happiness-suffering... birth-death cycle.

Is spirituality real? Is it beneficial to self-realization? Is it possible for a worldly person to be spiritual as well? Is spirituality tailored to a certain religion? Is spirituality asking us to be righteous? Is there any value to being spiritual in our everyday lives? This act of "thinking" starts a chain reaction. Thoughts wreak havoc on the mind. The mind enjoys fantasising about the past and daydreaming about the future in order to escape the current moment. This incessant loop of thoughts and lack of self-realisation subscribes us to sadness.

The Vedas are the oldest spiritual texts available to humanity. The Upanishads, on the other hand, are the series of spiritual-philosophical texts found embedded in the Vedas. The source of spiritual knowledge of the Upanishads is taken together to be called the Vedanta "Vedanta Nama" — Upanishad Pranam.

The word Vedanta means "the end of the Vedas," but it does not refer to the physical end of the books known as the Vedas, but rather to the final conclusion of the Vedas. The Bhagavad Gita is found in the Mahabharata. It is the dialogue between Krishna and Arjuna. But Krishna teaches Arjuna about spiritual life, and all the teachings are based on the Upanishads. Often, you find some of the languages of the verses in the Gita to be languages of the Upanishads. The philosophical discussion about the teachings of the Upanishads is found in aphorisms. The Vedantic idea of the human personality is trichotomous, i.e., body, mind, and consciousness [the real self].

ꟸ

There is a debate on the air about spirituality and its possible pragmatic practices. The word "Karma," though, is translated into English as "Work or Action," but not all work is considered Karma-yoga. When we say "work," different meanings are assigned to that one little word. Let's say, for example, motion is related to work. There is so much motion going on in nature. The sun, the moon, and even the giant water bodies or the wind are all whirling around in action. But can we consider that a work? No, I suppose. The big factory machines are going on for 24 hours... so is that karma? No, if I am not wrong.

Therefore, Karma is done by a living being in a living body. So the word karma, as it occurs in Karma-Yoga, relates to one work done by a living being, a living body, the sentient being that works. Second, it is a conscious business of ongoing action. There must be a sense of agency (the body), a sense of a feeling (the mind), or a sense of doer-ship (the individual) involved in the process of doing it. But if my good-guts are busy digesting the food that I ate last night, it is not considered work or karma being done. Why is it that there is no sense of doer-ship born out of this? So, now we know that Karma requires an agent to be consciously present in all actions. Third, there must be results associated with the work we are working towards. So the work we do and the results that we get, both good and bad, enjoyable and painful, are part of karma.

Unlike a machine that does a lot of work, it neither seeks enjoyment nor feels the suffering of doing it. And the same goes for the computer when it defeats human beings in a game of chess. The great chess grandmaster feels disappointed, depressed, and humiliated after working so hard to win and lose. Still, the coding behind the computer's intelligence does not feel triumphant at the loss or joyful at winning. The term "karma" does not apply to what the computer is doing but to what the grandmaster is playing. So there has to be agentship; there has to be an enjoyer or sufferer to pave the way for Karma.

The fourth consideration is a moral obligation. Karma has a moral dimension as well. Good or bad, righteous or unrighteous, these things become involved in the act of Karma. So, for example, a toddler may consciously or unconsciously do something, but what the baby does is not to be considered a good action or a bad action as he/she has not developed a sense of morality within the mind. Similar to animals, even if they do many things, for its consequences, you and I don't call the cops on the animal, which creates a nuisance, nor do we give up medals for their bravery, unless it's a defence dog who would save thousands of lives from the darkness of death.

Karma has a moral dimension that does not have to be present in all work activities. Again, the moral dimension has two parts. One is the morality of good and evil; the other is freedom of choice. If we think deeply about it, we will quickly realise that you and I cannot have good and evil unless we have free will. We could not praise a person for a good action done consciously or blame a person for a malicious action done consciously unless that thing was done freely. If a person is forced to do something terrible, you cannot really blame that person, and if that person unknowingly does something great, you cannot praise that person either. So, the moral dimension is there, and the moral dimension means that there must be good and evil, and the second is that there must be freedom of choice.

And finally, the last one is called the "cosmic result" or the "Karma-fala." This is usually how karma is understood in Sanskrit and many other Indian languages. When someone says, "My karma is terrible," we know that it is the inevitable results of our past karma that we are experiencing now. To mention the law of karma, Swami Vivekananda, in the "Song of Sannyasin", states: "good, good; bad, bad; and none escaped the law, but whosoever wears a form, there is the chain too..." So good karma eventually leads to good results, and good results mean pleasant things that tend to happen to you. In the sense of consciously committed immoral action, bad karma leads to unpleasant things.

As per the ancient Vedic scriptures, we have existed in the past, we have lived many lives before, and there we have done many things, and the results of our actions done in the past are bestowed upon us now. So that is called the result of our past karma. We are what we are now because of the many lives that we have already lived in the past.

The subject of four yogas covers the entire range of spiritual life. One way of understanding the four yogas is that spiritual life depends on how one perceives the problem. Karma yoga is the way of work or service; Bhakti yoga is the way of love and devotion. Raja Yoga is the way of meditation, and Jnana Yoga is the way of knowledge.

The solution to all these problems lies within themselves as the paradigms of spiritual awakening. In Karma-yoga, it is understood that the problem is selfishness, and the answer is unselfishness. Selfishness ties us to this little body and mind, i.e., this little personality known as "I Am." So all of my efforts in life, all of my work, all of my thoughts, and everything I do throughout the course of my days, months, and years are directed toward making this ambiguous "self" happy. Why is this primarily due to the fact that I have this body-mind identification? But we never question this horizontal "I." It goes without a question whether I am this thing called blood-flesh or something beyond this, as a doctor when he looks through an x-ray of the body and then identifies it as my ill body or my broken bones and every bit of this body. He just looked inside the body. He studied it all. I can see it in the pictures taken by x-rays, and yet I would wonder where in all of this the "I" is? The one who is thinking many thoughts, the one who is enjoying or suffering from the pain, the one who I call "myself." Where is this "I" in all of this? Each looks to me like a piece of this body. So is this the insight of this "I"? Or is there a subtler truth to be discovered about "who I am"?

The body, according to Advaita Vedanta, is the result of our 'Karma'—actions that we have put in motion in previous lives—and so generates this body of suffering and cravings. These activities are classified as "Dharma" and "Adharma," or "good" and "bad" deeds, respectively. Good activities result in pleasurable experiences, whereas bad actions result in unhappy ones, and we have this body to experience both. So this body is the result of our previous karma. Now the issue arises: why did we do any previous "karma" at all? According to true spirituality, we develop previous karma as a result of 'Raga and Dwisha.' In Sanskrit, Raga signifies want, yearning, clutching, pushing, and so on, whereas Dwisha represents hate and aversion. As a result, our "karma" follows the paths of desire and aversion. What causes "desire and aversion"? It is because of this duality that we experience in this world. There are things out there that I want, and there are things that I do not want, which I would rather avoid. So, pleasure and money, and fame and success, and health, long life, people in my life, relationships; we want these things. Failures, sickness, and death; who wants them? So, desire and aversion propel us through life and generate various karmas: good karma and bad karma. And 'Karma' gives rise to its effects. Finally, in this life, we have a body.

Babies can understand language much before they can speak. They can't talk, but they clearly understand everything said to them. So whatever the mother said, the baby understood. Take this as an example, and the story goes like this:

> *"There is one little baby named Aadya. She is travelling with her mother to her grandparents. While inside the car, her mother showed her the mountains, the trees, and the birds flying in the sky from the window, and baby Aadya would look around everything with big eyes and also offer it to her dad, who was driving the car. She is carrying a soft little toy in her hands. She calls it "Baby Bear," as suggested by her mother. And she would show it to her father with a big smile, and then the mother would show a picture of a baby girl on the mobile phone. It is the baby's picture on her mobile phone. When the mother asks, "Who is this? Baby Aadya turned to her father with a big smile and a proud look; she identified the picture and indicated it as "I" with her tiny fingers."*

Now, let us try and extract a very Vedantic insight from his simple story of baby Aadya. When she is shown the mountains, trees, birds, or even her baby bear, she rightly knows that all this is not her, not baby Aadya. But when she was shown a photograph of herself on her mobile phone, she could rightly recognise it. She did not say this is baby Aadya, as she said, "this is a baby bear, or that is the birds." Instead, pointing at the photograph, this 17-month-old baby Aadya said - 'I am this'.

The distinction between that and this is that the world and the body are automatically identified with the self-proclaimed "I". So we take this body and mind to be ourselves without question, and Vedanta, of course, says this doesn't seem right, and this is the root of "Samsara"... the world of illusion. And then we try our best throughout our lifetime to get rid of it.

The road to overcoming worldliness goes through the non-dual lane of spirituality. So this movement from selfishness to unselfishness; selfishness is the problem that traps us in the web of "Samsara" — the world of illusion and generosity is the only solution. This is Karma Yoga.

Among all the four yogas, Karma-yoga has something unique. This is the only one that is not private. Your meditation requires space, your devotion needs a belief, and your philosophy demands facts and understanding of the readings. All this belongs to you and is simply yours. It doesn't have too much to do with the world directly. One may get the fruit as one seed. But karma yoga is engaged with the world, with the public. Karma Yoga is a spiritual path directly in contact with the world. Hence, the result of one's righteous work is shared among all, and the consequence of all the evil works is shared with one too.

Another fact seen in today's world is that work is very important and for everyone. Whether one is in an ashram, in a family, or in a workplace, we are active, we are doing as many things as we can, and so we're coming into contact with people and with problems. Now, this takes so much time and energy that we cannot spiritualize our work-life. As a result, spirituality stands as a losing proposition. It will always lose. If we clearly make a distinction between our secular life and spiritual life, we see that out of 365 days, 362 of those days we are busy hunting around the world, either for something or for someone. Even with 24 hours in a day, how many hours are being spent practising spirituality? Maybe at the most, half an hour... On busy days, that time is reduced to no more than five to ten minutes. The rest of our time is best spent on accumulating wealth, eating all kinds of foods, sleeping an extra snooze hour, and pleasure-seeking. Meanwhile, most of our energies are invested in dealing with the world and our work, and only a little is left for spirituality. So, work also needs to be made more spiritual, or else the difference between the secular and the spiritual will lead to deep physical, mental, and moral insecurities in the future.

But Karma Yoga irradiates all of these insecurities and helps us to idolise a spiritual life without being religious or spiritual. It makes everything spiritual, even at work or doing any good deal of business, so much so that we can enjoy a guilt-free life.

Swami Vivekananda himself said that my mission in life can be put into a few words: "It is to preach unto humanity their inner divinity and how to make it manifest in every movement of life." He also said, "Each soul is potentially divine, and the goal is to manifest the divinity already within us." And one must do it through work, worship, philosophy, or devotion. Perform one or more or all of these and be free. This is the whole of religion. books, temple doctrines, churches‘ secondary details, and so on.

The keyword that we must pay attention to is "manifestation of the divinity already within us". So this is the first thing that Swami Vivekananda says: that there is a divinity potentially present within us. This is how he represents Vedanta, or the traditional Advaita Vedanta, to be very precise. And the claim is that we are one with absolute reality, the ultimate reality of the universe. There is an ultimate reality, and that ultimate reality is you. "TAT-TAMV-ASI" is the traditional formulation that we find in the Upanishads, "That Thou Art."

To be aware of the divinity within ourselves, one has to engage in a process of inquiry. But for obvious reasons, there is this body, and then, not just the body, there is this mind. Personality and spirituality teach us in various ways to inquire within ourselves. To inquire is to take a look at the inner-self. The Upanishads and the Vedantic texts tell us how to do it. So all you need is to listen to that and carefully track it, follow it in your own experience, and when you attend to your own experience, you will certainly realise the power of divinity within. This is known as the phenomenological approach.

The phenomenological approach means how reality appears to us right now, right here. It is quite distinct from believing in something that is somewhere else. For example, the idea of the higher heavens is a different kind of approach based on faith or devotion. There is also a mystical approach when you sit and meditate and you get extraordinary experiences, but the way of Advaita Vedanta is to attend to the experience that is now and here.

The experience of the subject and object, that is- I, being the experiencer, am experiencing the world as an object. While following this, we go inwards. I, the seer, become the subject and what I see is an object, which is the world. In this way, I look at the world as an object, I look at the body as an object, and I look at the mind itself as an object too. And these seem to be amazing new revolutions to us because we always thought, 'I am the mind in a body, that's it!' We never examine that, but then the mind itself is an object, or rather a series of subtle objects. We, with the approach of the seer and the seen, land on this idea that there is an awareness that exists at the core of our existence. That awareness is our real nature, but we can just say that my deeper nature is that awareness. It is easier to grasp than to immediately abandon that I am not the body, not the mind... I'm that awareness-consciousness. That's a little difficult. But let's say I, first of all, need to discover if such "awareness" is there or not. It has always been there.

There are five sheaths, or five layers, of the human personality. To start with, there is the physical layer known as the "Annamaya Kosha," or the food sheath. Inside that, there is a layer of prana, or life sheath... the "Pranamaya Kosha". Then there is a layer of thoughts, deeper and more subtle inwards to the body, which is the layer of thoughts, emotions, and memories that we identify with ourselves and we see that they are also objects, just like this body is an object. Those thoughts are also objects that are subject to continuous change, which is known as the "Manomaya Kosha," or "the mental sheath." Looking inwards, we find the layer of the sheaths of intellect which we are using right now to understand all these things is the "Vijnanamaya Kosha", the sheath of intellect and wisdom. Pushing inwards... further inwards there is the "Anandamaya Kosha", the bliss sheath which we get in the state of deep sleep, for example.

And as the knower, the observer, the illuminator, and the experiencer of these five sheaths, we experience the world as the unchanged "awareness-consciousness."

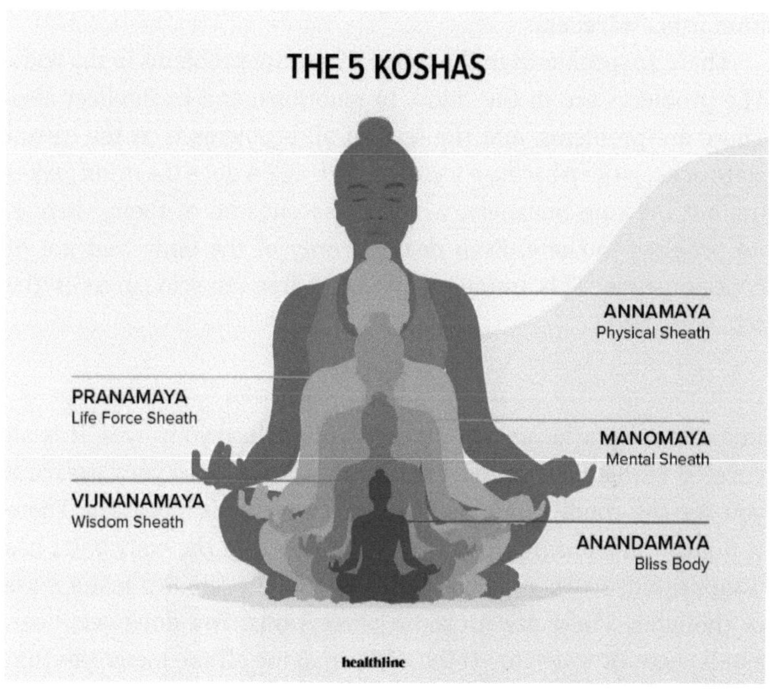

Layers to the Self ~ 'Atman' (Source - Google Images/Healthline)

In waking dreaming and deep sleep, the whole world goes away, and there's a world of dreams that go away, there is blankness. Not only is the world even more stunning, my physical body is going away. But, I, the self-proclaimed "Atman," am continually present there as the knower. It's remarkable and fascinating to imagine the nature of dreams where I continue as an experiencer, the knowing subject, and yet I have no idea of my body, not knowing whether it is lying on the bed or somewhere else. So that the world disappears before my eyes, the body disappears before my experience, and then it is replaced by dreams, which also disappear in the blankness of deep sleep, and then I wake up again. Through this method, I discover the same awareness that is experiencing all of this. This awareness is free of the world; it is free of the body; it is free of thoughts, feelings, memories; emotions; and personality. This is immortal awareness.

There are problems in the world. There are problems in the body. The problems are in the mind, in emotions, and in intellect also. There are problems, and the seed of all problems is in the causal state of deep sleep because it comes back again once the mind wakes up, but the consciousness, which transcends all of them, there is no problem in there. Even death is only of the body and not of consciousness. This immortal, problem-free consciousness is the self, you... and I.

Imagine the world outside disappearing before your eyes. It is all covered with snow and buried far away. Then close your eyes and you see the room where you are now slowly disappearing. There is nobody else around, and then you think that the body itself has disappeared. So, there is no physical body but remains just a mass of thoughts. There are no sense perceptions. You don't see, hear, smell, taste, or touch anything. Now imagine all the memories that you have gathered all throughout your life having disappeared and you being left with no memories, therefore, no mind. Imagine all your thoughts and ideas have disappeared and you are aware of the nothingness. Then you drop that nothingness also. And now you are just left with the light of awareness, which is always there, never gone.

So what is this awareness? What does it want? What does it need? What demands does it have? Nothing. It is perfectly fulfilled. It's always there, unmoving, unchanging, unnoticed. All the problems and demands and desires and lack of fulfilment come only when the mind starts working. Once the mind attends to itself, it activates the body and mind to the sense organs, and very soon the world reappears before us, webbing the net of suffering to happiness or happiness to suffering. Thus, impurity and purity come with the body and are raised by the mind. But, beyond the crisis of happiness and sorrow, the consciousness is always satisfied.

This is called the divinity of the soul. And this is what Swami Vivekananda meant by the statement he made, "Divinity within us". So, we already have it, but the whole point is to discover this reality of the divinity within.

Not only this, the second big thing which Swamiji taught in his great teachings about the self was: how many such divinities are there? One, two, or Manay? Our first reaction would be that, all right, if I am such an awareness, there would be many such "awarenesses" existing in the world. This plethora, or the plurality of awareness in all living beings, has been discussed by the Sankhyins. point of view. But Swamiji only talked about "the oneness of all existence".

In the Bhagavad-gita, Krishna says to Arjuna, "Know me alone to be the one awareness in all beings." Now look, even God is saying that this awareness which we now discover within ourselves is the same awareness which is present in and through all beings. That which is shining in and through all minds is God, and it is the "one and the same." It is the same witness-consciousness that knows everything but whom nobody knows. It is inside of us where the whole world is: the outside world is split into so many physical bodies, like waves in an ocean, that appear and disappear. This is what Swami Vivekananda calls "the oneness of all existence".

Swamiji's teachings roared like lions both in the West and in India. He built his philosophy on these two planks. One is the divinity within us, and the second one is the oneness of all existence. The divinity within each one of us is to be discovered in the oneness of all existence. If carefully noticed, he does not speak of "knowing the divinity within yourself" at all, but he emphasises "manifesting the divinity within yourself." According to him, he states, "My only ideal is to preach unto humanity; to revive their inner divinity and how to make it manifest in every movement of their life." Meaning, then, that in every move of life, how to show the reality of God in our thoughts, words, and actions is more important.

The manifestation of divinity does not only include the realisation of the body-mind to be an illusion, but it also flares out the other dimension of being absolutely fearless, owning love and compassion for everybody in society, unselfish services to humanity, self-discipline, self-control, and all such qualities of a saintly being soul should come into our lives. That is the full meaning of the word "manifest."

People would wonder, why does Swamiji use the word "manifestation" of the divinity already within us and not "knowledge" of the divinity already within us? So it must be expressed in the sense of ethical manifestation. Ethical manifestation is love for others, complete self-abnegation, complete unselfishness expressed in service, and fearlessness. These qualities of unselfishness, of strength, of fearlessness, of love for others, of control of the senses, must manifest even before self-realisation. Thus, he calls it a "full manifestation of divinity," meaning knowledge of the divinity and also the qualities that go along with it in shaping one's character.

Sister Nivedita, in her masterful introduction to the complete works of Swami Vivekananda, puts it so powerfully that instead of paraphrasing her words, I wish to quote them as originally spoken. She says, "All these things (which just now we read) would have been true even if Vivekananda had never lived. All of these Gitas, Upanishads, everything would have been there and remained authentic even if Vivekananda had not come, but he has given society and all of us something unique. We should never forget that Swami Vivekananda was the one who said that the Advaita philosophy is supreme because it includes the experience that everything is one without a second. His teaching philosophy is still better and easier to understand than any other doctrine that says the many and the one are the same reality that the mind sees in different ways at different times.

She further adds—"... its crowning significance to our master's life, Vivekananda, for here he becomes the meeting point not only of east and west but also past and future. If the one and the many are indeed the same reality, then it is not only all modes of worship alone that are paths of realisation, but equally all modes of work, all modes of struggle, all modes of creation. There is no distinction henceforth between sacred and secular; to labour is to pray, and to conquer is to renounce life. This is the realisation that makes Vivekananda the great preacher of Karma, not as divorced from but as expressing Jnana and Bhakti. To him, there is no difference between the service of man and the worship of God; between manliness and faith; between true righteousness and spirituality. All his words, from one point of view, can be read as a commentary upon this central conviction in human thought: that they coalesce into a force once in a while expressed in society.

For ignorance, the vaccine is knowledge. Swami Vivekananda says, "... from the serene to the yonder warm, there is one divinity shining through all. Therefore, we are all equal. The fight for racial equality and gender equality comes because we are struggling at the level of the body to establish equality. If oneness is the reality and all this difference is merely an appearance to the mind, then righteousness lies only in harmony. He adds, "There is no need to convert from one to many religions unnecessarily, because the religions of the world are not contradictory to each other. And as they are complementary to each other, we can all learn from each other to form a better world with the vision of oneness in the future.'

༄

The great difference between the ancient Greek and ancient Indian outlooks is that the ancient Greek outlook was that something would come out of nothing. So there's always the possibility of new things coming, and the new is always new and better, whereas the ancient Indian outlook was that something comes out of something. So whatever is coming, its roots are there and the source is behind it. The reality is that it's emerging from something that was already existing. Maybe that's the philosophy why, today, a new publication or new idea is more important.

The word "knowledge" means, by definition, new learning. Even in Vedanta, one of the terms used to define valid knowledge is "anadigata," i.e., that which has not been known earlier is now known. So knowledge is always new, whether it's in the east or the west. But what is meant in the Vedantic sense of knowledge being new is that when we study Vedanta and we practise spiritual disciplines, we get this new realisation. But it doesn't mean it's new in Vedanta, not even new for civilisation. It's always been there, but we now know it. In other words, knowledge is new for me only when I go to school and study the textbooks and attend the classes, but that doesn't mean it's new for the professor or for the discipline itself. It's been established and is well known in that sense. whereas the Indian tradition in terms of spiritual or philosophical knowledge has to be the expression of an established spiritual tradition.

Adi Shankaracharya goes so far as to say that the person who is not learned in the tradition, who does not know the tradition, even if this person has read all the books in the library, should be disregarded as a fool and doesn't know anything. In fact, these days, some modern spiritual teachers make radical claims to be bookishly spiritual. But they don't realise how utterly stupid and utterly discredited they may sound in the eyes of traditional learning.

The advantage of this modern approach is that the new must be better, and it must be more authentic. Maybe it's the model of progress in scientific knowledge where newer things are discovered and so the old things are just undiscarded, but that is not necessarily true or valid for spiritual knowledge.

Both sides have their advantages and disadvantages. The advantage of this modern approach is that there is always the possibility of a new discovery. There is always the possibility of a new and better approach in the so-called scientific world. There is always the possibility of adapting something to modern circumstances. Things change, and so knowledge must change accordingly, and that's the advantage. But the disadvantage is that they are often not worth the paper they are written on. By claiming to be new or to get it published, they make huge claims, and then when you see what is there, it's either a rehash of what is already there, or it is superficial, or it is just plain wrong. In the eagerness to be published, something new is not only not worth it, but it's a waste of time. That's the disadvantage.

The traditional approach again has its strengths and disadvantages. The traditional approach, even though it is the truth, is monotonous. A truth that is defined in the Upanishads or in the scriptures has been written and rewritten over a period of a hundred thousand years. The great disadvantage of this approach, of course, can clearly be seen as becoming uncreative and unoriginal after some time, just ornamental, i.e., to re-engineer the same gold into neckless, bangles, and rings. It might rob us of the power to think original thoughts.

The French philosopher, Michel Foucault, says, "The sun rises in the east, and this is a fact, but this is not the idea of truth-telling." According to him, truth-telling that is harmful to one's own selfish worldly interests is true, but if someone tells it without having the fear of being exposed, then he's told the truth.

The great Indian mystic and Swami Vivekananda's spiritual master, Sri Ramakrishna Paramhansa, said something similar ages ago. He says, "If a man can confess his faults openly to the world, then one must understand that there is some spiritual substance present in the man."

Like the Hindus, the Buddhists, the Jains, and all the other Indic religions, they do not believe in an eternal soul, the cycle of rebirth, or even in the existence of God, but they do all believe in the result of Karma and its Karmafala. As to that, Swami Vivekananda said, "... engaging with the world, going out into the world of plurality, but doing it ethically is the sign of religion. Whereas turning inwards, seeking the transcendental, and not being interested in worldly pursuits anymore is the higher spirituality.'

To believe in God is to believe in the law of karma. Being ethical and staying moral towards society is the sustainable way to live in this world. We cannot have a society without it, nor can we have an organisation without it, nor can we have a family without it.So all the churches, temples, and mosques are basically teaching this one sacred truth of having an ethical life. Having said that, there is a secret esoteric inner dimension that exists at the core of spirituality. Something that is beyond this world of morality and ethics, beyond the world of religion. Beyond all this, there is something higher to be achieved. Some call it "Nirvana", some call it "Moksha", some call it "Enlightenment", and some call it "Self-realisation or God-realisation." means the one and the same.

Thus, the purpose of Karma Yoga is "God-realisation," says Adi Shankaracharya in his commentaries on the Bhagavad-gita. Karma, or the work that is done in the path of religion, is moral action, ethical action. While the goal is still to attain success ethically, without cheating people, without destroying the harmony of family life or destroying the ethics of any corporate culture, living a good life morally is karma or "Dharmika Karma" (religious wellbeing), but it is also called "Sakuma Karma," i.e., karma is done with a certain desire. But in the higher religions or in spirituality, the role of karma becomes a Karma Yoga if only it is done without the desire for "Niskama Karma".

In Chapter 2, Verse 47 of the Bhagavad Gita, Sri Bhagawan says -

कर्मण्येवाधिकारस्ते मा फलेषु कदाचन।

मा कर्मफलहेतुर्भूर्मा ते सङ्गोऽस्त्वकर्मणि॥"

karmany-evadhikaraste ma phaleshu kadachana |

ma karma-phala-heturbhurma te sango'stvakarmani ||

You have the right to action alone. You never have the right to the fruit. Do not be motivated to act because of the fruit. But do not be motivated to not acting either.

[The above-mentioned translation was taken from Dr. Bibek Debroy's Unabridged version of the Bhagavad Gita. *Debroy, Bibek. The Bhagavad Gita. Penguin Books India, 2005.]*

Explanation: There are four things that Sri Krishna has told to Arjuna (represenataive of all human beings) through this verse certainly known as the central teaching of Karma-yoga : (a) You have the right to work, (b) You don't have the rights to the results of work, (c) Don't do thing for getting result/fruits of work, (d) Don't give up your work/action either.

It is wise to note two things here - work and the result of work are two saparate things. The outcomes of cause and causality designates the Law of Karma. Causes have causality or conscquences and the belife of causality is primiraly universal in nature. Therefore, the Law of Karma runs thus - good action deliberately done fruits in merit and the result of merit causes some pleasent occurances in life such as happiness, prosperity and peace. On the other side, bad action must ripe the result of inaction and unhappiness. So the law can be stated in this way ~ [Dharma = Punniya = Sukham; AND Adharma = Papa = Dukhham] Wc havc choice regarding Karma but we don't have the choice regardig the result. However, but very vagely this emplies that we have the power of freewill to choose our actions (only).

ꝏ

In the path of Karma-yoga, action is more important than inaction. In Bhakti-yoga, doing or understanding is not that important, but believing and having faith in God is. Moreover, karma, or action, has three effects. One is the immediate effect. Just as food satisfies hunger, When the hungry person is fed food, the hunger is removed immediately. It is a direct effect, and everybody sees it. The second is an effect of one's own mind. The habit of sharing with others gives us immense joy. The joy of doing good things for others creates a psychological effect in our minds. It's called 'Samskara' or righteous habits.

The third one is the law of merit and demerit. It results in some pleasant or unpleasant effects. So, the law is like this: "Dharma" good action consciously done leads to "Punnya" merit, and merit leads to "Sukha" happiness. Therefore, all the good things that are happening to us now and here are because of some merit we have and that we earned in earlier lives. But equally, all the unpleasant things happening to us are the result of your bad karma. It's us who have generated it with mighty energies subtly from the universe in some ancient time, because of which we are suffering now. So "Adharma" bad action leads to "Papa" demerit and demerit leads to "Dukhaa" unhappiness, and they are all limited. Consciously performed good deeds generate a limited amount of merit, which in turn generates a limited amount of nice things that happen to us, and vice versa.

Spirituality, on the other hand, is freedom from the cycle of merits and demerits, good and bad, paap and punniya. This worldliness is called "Samsara", the world of illusion. Swami Vivekananda's poem "good, good, bad, bad, and none escapes the law, but whosoever wears a form, wears the chain too..." Thus resemblance the cycle of karma.

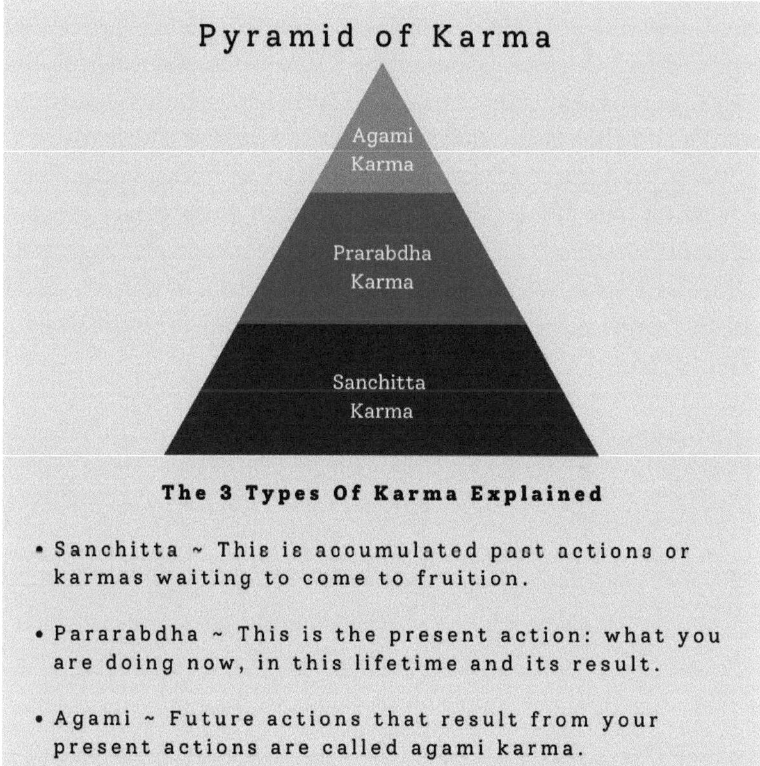

From the Vedanta perspective, this whole idea of Karma and Samsara could be decoded as follows: We are not aware of our infinite nature. This not being aware of the infinite nature of our divine nature is called ignorance. This ignorance then makes us feel incomplete. And therefore, we reach out into the world to do what appears to us just to complete ourselves. But in reality, there is nothing in the world that can complete us, nor do we need to reach out to the world for the same. But because of the darkness of ignorance, we do reach out to the world to compete with ourselves, and thus this reaching out is Karma: doing something for fulfilment. And as we do something, we set in motion this law of Karma, typically the result associated with cause and effect. We either do things well or badly, and that is how it leads to results perturbed by good and bad. Once we get entangled in the watch of our karma, the watch gets going and doesn't stop in one lifetime. Rather, it leads to innumerable lifetimes of people. Birth to birth. Death to death.

We get the result of our 'Sanchitta Karma' from the past lives to witness our "Prarabdha Karma" in the present and we are constantly accumulating "Agami Karma", the new karma that leads to further lives as well. Depending on the mixture of Karma—good or bad! Our lives are either pleasant or unpleasant, or more likely a fusion of both.

Problem	Soluation	Method
Impure Mind	Purity of thoughts	Karma Yoga
Restless Mind	Concentration	Bhakti Yoga & Raja Yoga
Ignoranent Mind	Knowledge	Jnana Yoga

Swami Vivekananda's take on Karma-Yoga

vs.

Problem	Soluation	Method
Ignorance	Knowledge	Jnana Yoga
Scatared Mind	Focus	Raja-Yoga & Bhakti-Yoga
Impure Mind	Pure Mind	Karma-Yoga

Adi Shankaracharya's take on Karma-Yoga

Even after attorning to everything in the material world throughout our lives, we can't honestly say that "Yes!" I've gotten what I wanted.The Gita says, by attaining "THAT," nothing greater remains to be attained; being established in "THAT," even the heaviest of sorrows cannot shake the one. So, have we got "THAT" figured out yet? That must be the question to ask within.

Now, in the age of proofreading, somebody who is an agnostic or someone who does not believe in these things might ask, "I know only this life." I don't know anything about my past lives, and I don't even know if I will have a future life. So what is the proof?

I agree with your propositions. Even if you forget all of this, there is still suffering in this life, which nobody can deny. There is unhappiness; there are problems in this world, but is there any deep solution to that problem? Spirituality promises that there is a deep solution to that problem. We can actually overcome suffering.

The nature of suffering is like a man hit by two arrows. One arrow led to suffering, and the second arrow caused even more suffering. Now, what are the two arrows? The first arrow is what the world throws at us. There is a natural catastrophe outside, like the COVID-19 pandemic. There are little personal tragedies that happen in life. There are some people around us who might be a source of our suffering. One's own body could be the main source of suffering too. Ultimately, all the suffering that comes to us is conceived only in our minds. So this is the thing that the world throws at us, which represents the first arrow. The second arrow is the suffering that we have inside as a reaction to the first arrow. While the first arrow is common to all beings, the second arrow acts differently for different beings. But the real cause of suffering is due to the reaction that one possesses in the mind, the second arrow. Unhappiness is actually more present in our minds than in nature.

'Spirituality though it cannot remove the first arrow or irradiates the suffering from the world that throws upon all of us it can convincingly remove the second arrow i.e. suffering of the mind inside ~ says the Buddha'.

Our real suffering is the second arrow, i.e., our internal suffering. It is not happening because of the world or even the body, but it is our whimpering mind that is continuously playing the song of mourning. And the whole significance of all the yoga's Karma, Bhakti, Raja, Jnana' aims at removing the second arrow from our lives.The practical aspect of practising karma yoga is to be achieved through these four approaches:

1	2	3	4
Work as the witness	Work for God	Surrender to God	Divive Play of God
Jnana/Knowledge	Bhakti/Devotion	Prapatti	Lila

The first is the Jnana approach, where one may work as a witness. Notice that everything is done by nature, and I am the conscious witness thereof. The work goes on; the body is working, the mind is working, and "I am the conscious witness of the working body and mind." The Bhagavad-Gita (Chapter 4, Verse 18) says: "The one who perceives action in inaction and inaction in action, that one is the wisest among all and that one is the doer of all action."

In the paradoxical language of the Gita, Sri Krishna explains the theme of karma to Arjuna on the battlefield. He says that there is something to be learned about both action (karma) and inaction (akarma).Whoever sees no work in work and no work in no work is truly seeing...The rational mind might analyse this as a silly statement that a wise person should see work as work. In the commonsensical approach, when someone does something, that's work, and when someone doesn't do anything, that's not work. Then how is it that doing no work is work and doing work is not work?

When the unwise person/when the ignorant person/when the unenlightened person says, 'I will give up work or I will give up karma (just like Arjuna when he wanted to stop doing his duty to fight against his cousin brothers) and sit quietly doing nothing, But that is also work. Because the doer is still pertaining to the rail of karma, being in a living body, having a sense of doer-ship or agency with a sense of enjoying or suffering under a moral obligation that includes choices to make followed by the cosmic result as shown in the table). If all those things are there, then clearly it is karma. So the wise person sees in the unwise person's decision to refrain from work that also works. That is also karma.

I'm on a fast.That means I am not eating, so that should be no work, but we take it as work, and it's a lot of hard work to observe a fast. If eating is work, then the practise of not eating is probably much harder work than simply eating. So the unwise person's decision to refrain from the activity is also an activity of a much worse kind, and the wise person sees that. And contradicting this, the wise person's activity is no activity at all. Would you like to question it? How? Because a wise person sees oneself as "Sakshi" consciousness and not as a body-mind engaged in action. So there is no sense of agency involved in his doings.

Consciousness is aware of the mind's thinking, it is aware of the senses engaged with the world, it is aware of the hands working or the feet walking... It is aware of all of that but clearly sees that being consciousness, 'I am not doing it..'

A true devotee would say everything is being done by the will of God, or an enlightened one who is not on the path of devotion would identify himself as the witness of what work is being done. Even if the enlightened one takes a lot of action, they can honestly say, "I did nothing." (Here the identification of the "I" is not the body and mind but the witnessing awareness that he or she really is...)

ꕤ

Adi Shankaracharya, in his commentary on the Bhagavad-Gita (chapter 4, Verse 18), says, "... just as a man crossing a river on a boat feels that the boat is not moving but the trees on the shore are moving. Similarly, the "Ajnani" (ignorant) state.It is the body and mind and senses which are moving and changing presented to his unmoving consciousness, but he feels, I walk, I talk, I think, I enjoy, I suffer... '

Truly speaking, nature does everything for us. Everything in this body and everything in the mind. From the digestion of food to the circulation of blood in the body, or the air being taken into the lungs and then pumped throughout the body, everything is done by nature.

Not even that, but even from our intention of raising the right arm to the actual execution of the task, so many neurons would have fired in the brain, so many things would have taken place in the nervous system and the muscles that are beyond the control of humans. Unless nature cooperates with the body-mind system, nothing can be done in the body.

Hypothetically speaking, if there comes a day when nature would say – Alright! You human's do think of yourselves to be so greatest invaders and you can run the body entirely by yourself right! So here are the keys! Go, drive the breath yourself...! Imagine then, one would simply die forgotten to inhale his breath. Our circulatory system, endocrine system, digestive system, nervous system if we are put in charge of all of that...imagine what will happen?

So, nature is a very reliable co-pilot and the ego within us says, "I am doing all this..." This is the web of the world (Samsara). It is nature that actually does all of the activities in this body, and I (we) are the witnesses thereof. In the Gita, there is a sloka that is repeated three times, stating the same thing. Everything is done by the gunas of nature, Satva, Rajas, Tamas, and the self, deluded by the ego, I am the doer".

In the 13th chapter of the Bhagavad-Gita, it says, "Nature alone does everything, and the person who sees this sees that the self is the non-doer." And again, the same remark is made in the 18th chapter. So, this first approach to karma yoga is mentioned three times in the Gita as "witness-consciousness."

ઇ

The philosophy of Swami Vivekananda's was simple like that. He used to say, "My God the poor, my God the hungry, my God the ill, my God the wicked!" he said! And we should serve them through education, through food, through medicine and treatment, through kindness and compassion. To go out of your way to be helpful and be nice to people. Therefore, never approach anything except as

God. So, that is the worship of God in all beings by converting our work into the worship of God. Sri Ramakrishna Paramhamsa says, "Hold on to God with one hand and do the work with the other, and when the work is finished, hold on to God with both your hands'

Swami Madhabananda Maharaj Ji writes: – 'I consider that the way Swami Vivekananda has advised us to worship God in man or to worship man as God is Bhakti-yoga. As soon as you have the idea of worship, it is no longer remains confined to the sphere of karma, not even Karma-yoga. We can call it "Bhakti-yoga." Before the beginning of any work or anything you want to do or to drive from here to there, in the beginning, take the name of God, chanting—'Oh! My Lord, I offer this to you'. During the work, mentally worship the Lord and, after the work is finished, offer the outcome of the day, good or bad, to the feet of the Lord.

There are 20 practical points to follow in Karma-Yoga given by Swami Birajananda Ji Maharaj as follows:

"*1. Other than karma-yoga, all yogic paths imply spiritual practise in solitude. Karma-yoga alone has the power to bring the spiritual ideal directly into the busiest field of life struggles.*

2. The goal of Karma-Yoga is one's own liberation and the welfare of the world. Do all the work with this twofold end in view.

3. Perform all work as either service to God, who dwells in all beings, or as participation in cosmic sacrifice. That is to say, all work must be done either with devotion to God or with knowledge of self. Either way, the important point is to make karma a means of connecting individual life with universal life.

4. Consider all people to be potentially divine, but do not confuse potentiality with actuality. It is undeniably true that God exists. is present in all beings, but that does not underrate the reality and power of evil. Despite the fact that the one divine dwells in all.The manifestation of divinity is not the same for all. In the sinner and the saying, "God dwells," be careful of the sinner. So we have to be careful in dealing with evil-minded people and difficult situations.

5. Every day, we should spend at least half an hour in silent contemplation in the morning and evening.The danger of karma-yoga is becoming extroverted or being in a state of busyness. One must learn the value of pulling back from the world, and this is especially important for Karma Yoga. Busyness is not spirituality. One of the tests of progress in Karma-Yoga is the attainment of purity of mind. Another test is the reduction of stress and strain. If instead of making the mind pure and freeing it from tension, work makes it more and more impure or increases mental tension, In such a situation, there must be something wrong with the way work is being done. "Way here means one attitude to life..."

6. In karma yoga, what matters is not what we do but how we do it. In karma-yoga, there is no distinction between lower and higher work, between secular and sacred work. All work is sacred. (As there is a Bengali saying goes, "from mending shoes to chanting the scriptures, all of it is spiritual.")

7. Choose the type of work that is in harmony with your temperament. (As a result, resistance will be reduced...)If you have no freedom to choose your work, try to make whatever work you are asked to do meaningful to you. That is somehow connected to God or spirituality.

8. Make your outer life an expression of your inner life. Let your whole life be an undivided consecration to the ideal. (It is not that when I am into meditation, then I am spiritual and the rest of it is boring business. It is absolutely not like that. Worshipping in your meditation room is as spiritual as working in the office, or service to the community, or taking care of the family. Thus, all of our lives and work become worship.

9. Whatever you do, make it a good one.Be efficient at work. Avoid sloppiness, bungling, and wastage of time. These are signs of Tamas and Rajas. Karma-yoga demands a sattvic mind.

10. Always prefer collective welfare to self-interest. (Karma-Yoga will always prefer collective welfare to self-interest). In the name of service, do not exploit other people, especially the poor. Unless one has the spiritual goal in mind, very soon, social work also becomes selfish work.

11. Never go against your conscience.Do not do anything that lowers your self-respect. Have high self-respect without being egoistic (the symbol of a karma-yogi)

12. Make service a way of life. Do service not as a duty but as a natural way of life. Service calls for sacrifice; always be ready for sacrifice. (The idea of servant-leadership, popularised by Robert Greenleaf. He has a whole foundation for servant leadership, saying, "Our ideals should be service, which is service, and when you get a position of leadership, you use that for service." But when you're not in a position of leadership, you still go on serving because the primary identity is and should only be service. So servant-ship flows into leadership, and if leadership comes, it is very good, but once it goes away, the servant-ship remains current and continuous. Don't wait for the opportunity, the power, and the resources to serve others.

13. A service that did not begin with an idea but with a feeling is the real meaning of service.

14. Karma-Yoga is not necessarily a technique for attaining success in worldly life. The purpose must not be about success but service. Karma-Yoga is spiritual. It's not meant to make a million dollars or even get the Nobel Prize or something like that. It may or may not happen, but that's not the point of service or action.)

15. A Karma-yogi must always maintain mental equanimity in the face of success and failure, praise and blame, and remain calm.There must be a sense of forbearance.

16. Do not blame other people for your troubles or failures in life. 17. The attitudes and behaviour of other people towards us depend on our attitudes and behaviour towards them.

17. In the field of work, one of the main problems is getting along well with one's superiors, with one's equals, and with one's subordinates or juniors. Some people adjust themselves very well to superiors but find it difficult to adjust to equals and juniors, whereas some people get along very well with their equals and juniors but find it difficult to adjust to their superiors.

18. Time management is an important aspect of Karma-Yoga. A karma-yogi should do all the work at the right time and within the shortest possible time. Reading newspapers, novels, watching TV shows, and unnecessary chatting, which is very common now among people who are engrossed in the internet, not only wastes time but also reduces efficiency and concentration.Sticking to a strict daily routine is a great help in proper time management.

19. Always remember, in external dealings, to act in accordance with place, time, and person, and to avoid being stubborn.

20. In practical life, the real task is to combine work and worship together."

The Way of Love

III

Invocation

"There will always be a need for something. Let's be SOMEONE first!"

Veer and Neel were childhood buddies who used to play and fall ill together after mud-dancing in the rain for long hours. They were, in fact, longtime friends. They've spent their entire lives together and have the best family relationship possible. Both of their fathers worked for the same government agency, and their mothers were good old friends. They have studied at school since pre-school. As it turned out, Veer had forgotten to bring a copy of his assignment from his English instructor the day before, and when the teacher asked for it, he failed to provide it. As a consequence, the instructor made him stand in front of the whole class in his chair and told him that he would be punished if he did not stand until the conclusion of class. When Neel saw his buddy being treated unfairly, he stepped up and claimed it wasn't his fault; Veer gave him his homework copy since it was Neel who hadn't completed his homework. The instructor motioned for them to both sit down. He also urged them not to make the same mistake in class again, but he admired the depth of their friendship's honesty.

From that level of pre-schooling up to the last day of their school, they happened to be together, helping each other in the study business, praying for each other's success and celebrating it the same way. They have always made their parents happy and proud of their success in their studies. Both of them have scored the same result, and they have also been awarded by the teachers of the school for scoring well. And now they were about to take up their school journey ahead on the college campus in the next few months.

Like the darkness of a bright light that stands just behind on a New Year's day, the untimely death of his father takes away all the smiles from Jay's family. The father of the family died an unfortunate death, leaving behind the only son and his mother with undifferentiated pain and toughness. The father had saved some money that they couldn't afford to feed their fate and soothe their stomach for a few days. And so a bad time had rained down on Veer's life without an early call.

Veer's mother wanted him to fight back against their fate and asked him to study hard to achieve the dream that his father had dreamt of him every day. The father wanted to see his son reach the heights of success but never lifted his feet off the ground to be humble. The death of his father had not just brought them down into insufficiency, but it had also issued a whole lot of unchanging challenges to be faced in the society that it usually demands. Many social parents do not allow their sons to play with fatherless boys, even on a good and sunny evening. It had constructed a great wall between the rich and the poor for a long time. Some people want to be rich and famous, but they can't protect their basic humanity; if there is an untimely widow, a poor mother, or a fatherless son, they don't deserve any kind of help from other people or money.

Neel went off to study abroad to peruse his further education and had decided to settle his future there, and that's how the line of friendship between Veer and Neel ended up without a hint. After a successful funeral ceremony for his father, Veer joined a basic government college and resolved to continue his studies there until he could earn some riches for his only parent. His mother decided to serve in the Shiva temple as a cook, and has devoted herself completely to the feet of the universe. In a way, both the son and his mother find their lives safe under the surveillance of Shiva, the Lord of the Universe (Ishwara).

Veer welcomes all the new challenges in life, accepting them the way they come in hand as the grace of Shiva. He was well aware that nothing could be more difficult or worse than this; he may have lost his father's hand from his head, but he had received the feet of the almighty to live and lead. Life loves to play with each and all at some point in time, but if the root is strongly grounded on the earth, no matter how cruel the windstorm strikes, it can put him down on the ground, but it can never take him off the ground. He can always stand up strong and still against his bleeding feet and look back hard for survival.

IV

All in One, One in All

The subtlest things often turn out to be the most difficult things to do, and spirituality is the most subtle of them all. People do say that spirituality is in the mind and that no external things are required. This is true, but at the subtlest level of the mind, it is very difficult to hold on to something without knowing the externality of the mind—Time, Space, and Form. When the external conditions are well understood and properly known, instead of moving around here and there, sit near to the holy shrine in a pure place for a specific period of time to focus the mind on God's spirituality. Bhakti, or devotion, is the journey of the self toward the self from the outside world to the inside world.

There are practical and philosophical grounds for the worship of God. "The reality of non-duality doesn't contradict the experience of duality." One big source of misery in spiritual life is the wrong conception that if we are concerned about ourselves, then we will be happy. Often, this selfishness or self-obsession becomes the greatest obstacle to happiness. Swami Vivekananda stated that "Those who live for others; the rest are more dead than alive." People who serve others are far superior to selfish self-seekers. For true happiness, the Bhakta's [devotees] often sing: "Forget the future, remove the past, and fill up the present by chanting the name of the Lord."

All of us were born with a certain bandwidth of attention. The more we can focus on that bandwidth into the object of concentration, the more focused and concentrated we feel. But if we choose to give only a little bit of our cognitive capacity to focus on the object of concentration and leave the rest of it free to roam around in the wilderness, it will think of many other things. When the mind thinks of many other things, all of which would be more attractive than the real work, then you and I feel the task is too boring, unpleasant, and difficult. And the only way to engage our minds in something is by putting our minds into a habit of active concentration.

All the knowledge that we have, either of the external or internal world, is obtained through only one method: concentration of the mind. No knowledge can be had of any science unless we can concentrate our minds on the subject. The astronomer focuses his thoughts through the telescope... and so on. If you want to study your own mind, it will be the same process. You will have to concentrate your mind and turn it back upon itself. The difference in this world between mind and mind is simply the fact of concentration. One, more concentrated than the other, gets more knowledge. (The source is Swami Vivekananda's talks at Washington Hall in San Francisco on March 16, 1900.)

In Bhakti-yoga, the puja [worshipping of God] or chanting [repeating the holy name of God] does engage the cerebral faculties of the mind and makes it more focused on the wealth of devotion to God. It gets easier and easier, so you don't have to struggle at a very subtle level, where you and I would have to use the more powerful aspect of our real nature—"Ayam Atma Brahma"—to make it happen. This self (the Atman) is Brahman (God). [One of the Mahavakyas] in the Atharva Veda's Mandukya Upanishad. a

ꟾ

"This is nice and that is not, and I must have it... I must enjoy it... I must see it... I must get it by all means..." As such, our desires are completely based on worldly attractions, and hence they flow outward all the time. So our desire to sense objects is the cause of all our problems, and the solution is to take all that desire and focus it on God, which is called "Bhakti-Yoga." In Bhakti-yoga, the desire stays, but now it is redirected to the innerwardness of the heart. The same "I want the world" [outer] becomes "I want God" [inner]. Thus, giving up the world and completely changing the focus to God is the real teaching of "Bhakti-yoga." If our problem is desiring the world, then the solution described in Bhakti-yoga is to turn the flow of the worldly desire around and focus it on God. That is devotion [Bhakti]. The Raja-yoga paradigm [meditation] is that all my thoughts are scattered about the world, and because my thoughts are scattered, the spiritual truth is not revealed to me. The problem is, as the Raja-yogi says, the problem is not whether you want God or not, whether you're selfish or unselfish. The problem really is that our minds-are unsteady. They keep flickering. They are scattered. If we only focused our minds, then the truth would be revealed to us. So, from scattered mind to focused mind; from mind scattered in the world to mind gathered and focused on God... whatever you call it! From the unmeditive mind to the meditative mind, that is, from problem to solution, that's the raja yoga paradigm. The Jnana-yoga, or the path of knowledge, is the paradigm that says the problem is ignorance. We do not know who we are. The issue with who we are right now, right here, is that it is referred to as ignorance, and the solution to ignorance is knowledge. So from ignorance to knowledge is the Jnana-yoga paradigm. From scattered mind to concentrated meditative mind is the Raja yoga paradigm. The Bhakti-yoga paradigm is the change from mind desires that flow out into the world to mind desires that are all focused on God.

The divinization of human relationships is actually the way of Vedanta. Swami Vivekananda said that the way we approach God in Vedanta is that we "humanize our relationships with the divine and divinize our relationships with the human." What does that mean? Our relationships with humans revolve around father, mother, husband, wife, children, friends, and so on, and our relationship with God is something very high and divine. But Vedanta reverses this relationship. The relationship that we have with humans as father or mother is it possible to perceive that relationship with God? Can we see God as the father? Can we see God as a mother, or can we see God as a child? And with human beings, the people around us, instead of just seeing them as other human beings or little limited persons with flesh and blood, can we see the divinity in them?

So that is what is meant by "divinizing our human relationships. Seeing God in everybody and humanising our divine relationship with God as God my father, God my mother, God my child, God my friend... like that. This teaching of Swami Vivekananda is known as Bhakti yoga—the path of love and devotion to God.

Swami Vivekananda says that most of what we think of as spiritual practice, such as singing hymns, offering ritualistic worship to God in images, icons, and repeating the name of God in temples, churches, and mosques, is preliminary. All of it is meant for the purification of the mind. But one thing stands alone as advanced, and that is when genuine love for God grows in the human heart. That is spiritual. That is advanced spirituality.

And of all the things that purify the mind, Swami Vivekananda says, the most powerful is renunciation, or "Tyaga." When one turns away from most of the non-sense that occupies our days and nights, and our hearts turn to God from the illusion of "samsara," that's the core idea of renunciation.

Of all these methods of purification that ultimately culminate in one action, the most powerful purifier is "Tyaga". In the Vedas, it is said that "renunciation" is the only way some people have become immortal.

Renunciation does not mean giving up everything that we may possess in the world around us, nor does it take anything away from us. However, each type of yoga requires renunciation. Swami Vivekananda says it clearly in his teachings on Karma yoga. He says that in the path of karma, or action, our actions do not change, we do not change. We continue to do the work in the office and at home, and we perform rituals in the temples in much the same way they used to be. But what makes our karma turn into karma yoga is only when our work is transformed from "Sakama Karma to Nishkama Karma," i.e., from selfish action to selfless action, then it becomes Karma-Yoga.

Just as so, when the purpose of doing anything is not limited to only gaining for oneself but shifted to the welfare of all beings and in the worship of God by giving up the fruits or results of gaining. However, giving up the fruits doesn't mean that you'll return your salary check for the sake of unselfishness. That would be highly idiotic. It means now you're not doing it for the sake of it anymore. Your whole goal is oriented towards being selfless and as an act of devotional worship to God. This is giving up the fruits of action in the language of the Gita. And it's an enormous act of renunciation. Not very easy, but certainly not too difficult either. People collect things like names, fame, money, power, and appreciation in order to feel good about themselves. But do these things really make people happy?

Everything that we gain for this little person is soon to be found unsatisfactory at some point in time. The old body will not learn to appreciate a new Tesla car, and the very cluttered mind is only seeking pills to declutter it at night.

In that case, the teaching of Bhakt-yoga frees us from the mesh of a decluttered mind to the mist of self-love and into love and devotion to God. If we do something unselfishly for others, thinking as if we are worshipping God, we will find the real satisfaction, we'll actually find the real fulfilment in life we have been looking for so long and so forth. But it comes with a price of renunciation, no doubt.

The philosophy of Sankhya says, "that which is awareness and that which you are aware of; these two are distinct entities." This stepping back from the whole of nature, from the whole of "Prakriti," is a great act of giving up. In the light of the first mantra of the Isha Upanishad, Adi Shankarachrya says, "I see one God everywhere." [Brahma satyam, jagat mithya, and jivebrahmava naparah] But this is to be realised and be centred on by the 'Tayaga' renunciation. " Renunciation of what? And Shankaracharya further commented on the same mantra, saying, "Do not covet anybody else's wealth because there is no wealth to be coveted. It's an appearance... it's a mirage. So, what will you covet if it doesn't exist in reality? "

Now, imagine the kind of renunciation that is being asked of us. At the point that we may begin to understand the slice of spirituality in the context of Advaita's non-dual philosophy, we are pretty much asked to understand that this entire world, which appears before us, coating all the good and the bad in it, and this body, which is so precious to us, that which portrays our basic identity and our personality, even that, is merely an appearance in consciousness and hence it's not real. The underlying reality is "Sat-Chit-Ananda" existence-consciousness-bliss as we truly are.

In contrast, Swami Vivekananda points out that "bhakti" literally means "in the way of devotion and love." This renunciation has become much easier to accomplish. One does not even notice when s/he has renounced the entire world just by closing their eyes before God with one-minded devotion. The happiness and fulfilment that one may receive from renouncing the world for God, as if the heart is blazing with the joy of love, are truly unconditional.

Swami Vivekananda gives four examples that confirm how renunciation becomes easier in Bhakti, in the way of love. First, he takes the example of the human relationship of love and longing. To paraphrase it for simplicity, I have the chance to write it this way: when a man falls in love with a woman or a woman loves a man, they fall out of love. And after some time, they fall in love with somebody else again. So, once we fall in love with somebody else, we tend to loosen up the earlier relationship for the advancement of our new bond, and very soon the old emotions disappear from the air [if not completely, but still] because now we are in love with somebody else.

The second example he gave us is of nationalism. So a person loves themselves. On the one hand, for him, it is only I, me, my, mine, my own family... and that's it. Then it expands from one's community to one's nation. Nationalism is a great power. The devotion to one's nation, which can inspire a person to give up his/her life, is largely witnessed by all of us. It is a love for the vast, a love for the nation. But further, one might expand beyond the narrow lanes of nationalism to include all of humanity. Outgrowing the love for nationalism to humanity doesn't feel like giving up on anything, but it feels like we have grown bigger, better, and more fulfilled in the real sense of existence.

Third, he discusses the crazy ply of the senses. He says, in order to see something nice, to taste, to touch, to smell, to hear, the things of the senses pull us, and we are mad after getting them almost blindly. But as we grow up, we get smarter and smarter and change our habits from big and obvious to small and subtle. Our senses will become more active, making it easy to get rid of the weird ones.

Let's say if somebody had cultivated a taste for classical music, the joy in it would be so much higher, so much more refined, and so much better than if they spent hours and hours listening to a difficult rendition of a particular piece of classical music in loops. It will not make them feel like they have given up or renounced anything, but that they have gained everything else that one may wish for. So, how has this person moved from enjoying the lower things of the senses to enjoying the higher things? It's because the joy is so much more refined and higher in terms of rendering the right one. He does not feel he has given up anything but feels he has gained much more, and this is renunciation of the senses.

And at the end, one more very beautiful and simple example that Swamiji has given us is that in the deep of the night, the only source of light are the twinkling stars in the sky. But when the moon rises, it sort of overwhelms the starlight. Quite similarly, when the sun rises in the morning, the beautiful full moon, which is still there on the horizon and sometimes can be seen parallel to the sun; the moon, which was so glowing in the darkness of the night, is overwhelmed by the sunlight and is now just faintly visible in the day time.

Similarly, when the love of God arises in the human heart, all the pull of the senses which were so powerful earlier, the illusions and delusions of worldly relationships and worldly commitments, all become like the dim starlight or even like the faded moonlight which has been cast away, overwhelmed by the light of the sun. So, this light of the love of God arises from within.

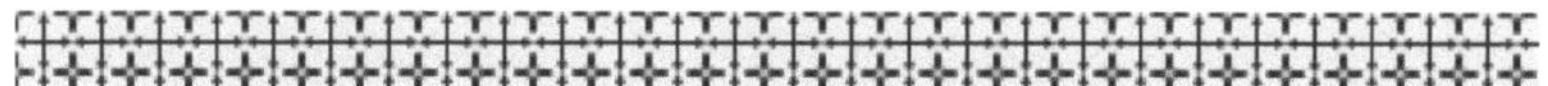

The second approach is in the path of bhakti-yoga, in which everything in this universe belongs to God, and I am here to serve. So all my actions are transformed into worship.

There is this monk who is passing through the security check-in at an airport. A security guard asked him, "Sadhu Maharaj, please tell us something of the secrets." The monk is making transit to get onboard his next flight. The monk was frisked and forced to stand on top of a mettle box by the security guard. The security guard, after the security check, requested the monk to give them a quick talk. He then called for all the cops around him at the airport. All the policemen and women stood around the monk holding guns in their hands to listen to his talk.

"Do you do puja before you leave your house?" the monk asked. And the gentle policeman said, "Yes! Before I leave the house for my job, I put flowers at the feet of Lord Hanuman. The monk then said, "Every day when each person files past you throughout the day, you must check the person very efficiently and very politely as part of your duty, and with every passenger that passes by, you mentally put one more flower at the feet of Lord Hanuman."

With a delighted smile, the policeman said, "Wah! Sadhu Maharaji! Like this, the whole day I will be worshipping my lord. '

The beauty of "bhakti," or devotion, is that not one human emotion has to be given up in the pursuit of love and the attainment of God. In the words of Ramakrishna Paramhansa, he says, "To complain in spiritual life is not considered as spiritual, but if you complain to God, against God, with God, that is as spiritual as prayer." Have you or I ever asked, "How do we gain undivided attention to God from the constant chattering of the mind?" And if we look for the answer outside, I am afraid it'll be given to any one of us any day soon. There is an old Indian saying that goes like this; at least in Bengali, it states: "Bise Bish Kate" (the poison is removed by the poison alone). Therefore, we may apply the same medicine to vaccinate our minds. So, the most effective way to make the mind stop chattering is to chant the name of "Sri Hari," the God to God. Hence, talking with God will overcome talking with the mind. In the flowery path of 'Bhakti', every emotion can be directed to the love of God. Seeing God in everything... be it an object or being. It is the silent mind that could sing the song of love just like the monk in devotion to God, and this is the beauty of the path of "Bhakti."

Swami Vivekananda, whose greatness is unfathomable from beginning to end, gives a unique insight into Bhakti. He says, "Hari," the name of God quite commonly known in the Vaishnava traditions in India (the Hare Krsna's). So, "Hari" is the one who attracts and takes away all the pain and emotions from our mind-heart. And there is this one force, says Vivekananda, which is working in the entire universe, everywhere. It is the same force that drives a mother to love her baby and make endless sacrifices to raise a child, and it exists not only in human society but also in the animal kingdom. It is the same driving force, the same love of God,

"Sri Hari." " It is inspired by that higher love that somebody goes out to make money to fulfil his ambition and desire to be rich... Even the notion of greed, which is quite a lower manifestation of the same supreme energy that brings us disappointment and frustration if it is not directed towards God. It is God alone who is pulling us, but deluded by a froth of ignorance, we do not see the truth and partake of it as if it is money that pulls us nearer. Not just money; even the power associated with success is the same love of God, disguised as power. But we think that if we get that powerful position, then we'll be fulfilled. Happiness is only in attaining God.

The novelist who spends hours and hours, day after day, every day writing his/her bestseller novel, or the painter who spends a whole lifetime pouring time and energy into colouring his/her art... even that urge is the same cosmic love working through those channels. It is the love of a billionaire who, after accumulating all the wealth in society, turns charitable and wants to do something for society and pours that wealth back into society for the same love. That is the vision of Swami Vivekananda for the entirety of love. He sees that our love for God is actually God's love for us. So, it is God's power of attraction working through us all the time. It is the true devotee who recognises the truth about this force, which is the love of God. And Swami Vivekananda says, "The devotee avoids all the friction and conflict, knowing that every one of us is being propelled by this force." Whether we love somebody or fight against somebody, it's the same force. All our desires, anger, etc. are propelled by the same force. But all of it is misdirected because we do not recognise its source. We do not recognise that it is God who is pulling us. Only a genuine "Bhakta" devotee... The lover of God recognises this truth and avoids all this trouble, all this friction, and goes straight to the source. An ignorant person, not knowing this truth, thus wanders from dream to dream... from mistake to mistake.'

The Austrian neurologist and the founder of psychoanalysis, Sigmund Freud, and Swiss psychiatrist Carl Jung, thought they had recognised that there was this one force from which many human activities were functioning in their "libido-mortido" theory, but the very mistake they made by calling it "the fundamental." Even the fundamental is also a manifestation of that ultimate original cosmic attraction, i.e., the attraction of God. This tremendous vision is the vision of "Bhakti," of cosmic love, and only the devotee recognises this truth.

ഋ

Sri Ramakrishna Paramhamsa would say, "People cry bucketful for their wives, children, and money, but nobody weeps for God." People are mad at the world, and I'm also mad, but I choose to be mad at God. Bhakta's renunciation is a renunciation of love. "Bhakti" devotion does not demand giving up anything or the world, but is urged to love God more and hence find the entire world within. Go towards the "east" and eventually the "west" will fall behind. The more you go towards God, the more the world of "Samsara" falls behind you. (Here, "east" represents devotion, and "west" represents godless desires.)

In the battle of Kurukshetra, Arjuna asks this question to Sir Krishna (Bhagavad-Gita: Chapter 12, Verse 1): The path of knowledge you have taught me and also the path of love. Which is better?

Arjuna asked, "There are devotees who are always immersed in you and worship you, and there are those who think of the unmanifest and the indestructible" (impersonal pure consciousness). Who among these is the best yogi?

And Krishna answers unambiguously in the Bhagavad-Gita: In Chapter 12, Verse 2, he says, "Those who worship me with minds fixed on me and always united in me with supreme devotion in my mind are the best yogis." [***This paragraph is curiously taken from Dr. Bibek Debroy's unabridged translation of the Bhagavad-Gita***]

So, the one whose heart is set on God in love and in devotion is undeniably the better yogi. The main difference between the path of knowledge and the path of love is that on the path of knowledge, we by default end up feeling that we are bodies with consciousness. The modern science of consciousness study is mostly stuck in thinking we are a body with consciousness, and they call it "the hard problem of consciousness." Whereas the truth is very straightforward and simple, we are consciousness alone in which this body-mind appears as one beam of "that" effulgent light. In the Advaita Vedanta, it just reverses the saying, saying "you are consciousness experiencing a body."

In the commentary of the 'Bhagavad-Gita', Ramanujacharya paradoxically says: "enlightenment is possible if we have controlled the senses; if you are enlightened, then only you can control the senses." So it's a vicious circle. Without perfect control of our senses, we cannot make the breakthrough to realise that we are beyond the senses... beyond the mind. But without making that breakthrough, we really can not control the senses. From the Kathoponishads, it says, "based on the witness consciousness, which is beyond the body, beyond the senses, beyond the mind and intellect, from that perspective, now controls the "body-mind-intellect". But the biggest question here arises as to how to perceive that perspective of controlling the senses in the first place. To answer that, Ramanujachrya says, "... control of the senses is much easier if you have 'Bhakti'. That which is lovable for the senses, instead of stopping them forcefully, directs them to the love of God and feels one with the universe. So, in Bhakti-yoga, stepping back from the sensory engrossment is much simpler and direct.

Our ignorance of the supremeness of God is at the level of intellect. To eradicate ignorance, we require knowledge, which too comes at the level of the intellect, because knowledge is a function of the intellect and it removes ignorance. But at the stepping-stone level of our personality when it is not well integrated, it is the desire for the world that keeps us flowing towards the world that is not an intellectual desire. All that stays at the level of the heart and emotions. Bhakti then works at that level.

If the form of the desire is "I want the world," what Bhakti does is maintain the same "I want," but instead of the world, it puts god there. So that one can continue wanting, one can continue desiring, one can even continue to be greedy, but all that is now connected to the pursuit of God. This is the practical acquaintance of "Bhakti"—the path of love. Another insight of 'Bhakti' according to Swami Vivekananda, he calls it the 'Triangulum of love'.

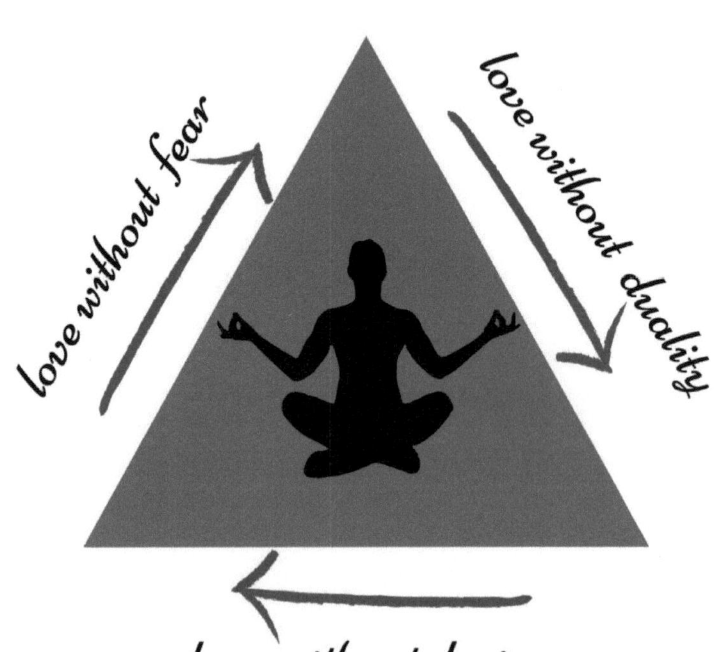

The higher stages of development in the way of 'Bhakti" by Swami Vivekananda

1. 'Shraddha' or Respect for God
2. 'Preeti' or Pleasure in loving God
3. 'Viraha' or Feeling the absence of God
4. 'Sansthana' or Thinking but only of God
5. 'Tadiyata' or Belonging to God

This is the way of love in which the lover and beloved, i.e., the human and the divine, are merged into one radiance of love.

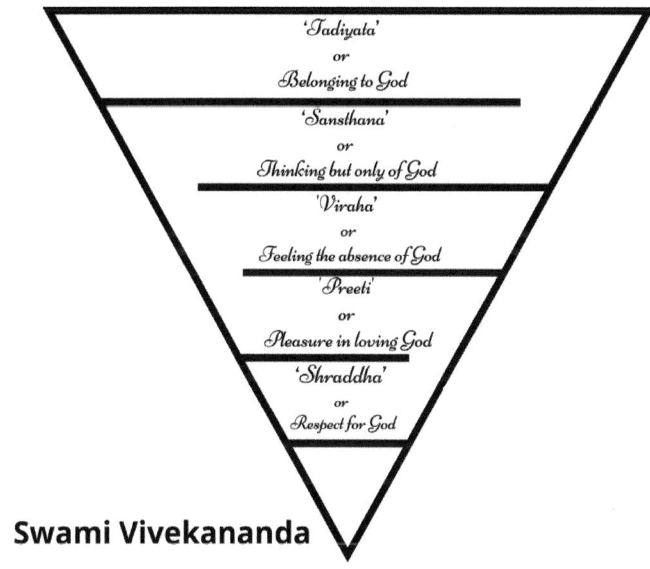

So, a religion may begin with the fear of God, but devotion only requires the love of God. Swamiji puts it very beautifully, saying "many come to an understanding; only a few realize..." Let thy lover, love, and beloved be that one blazing light until it is revealed to be God, the "one in al," the "al" in one.

Tying the mind down in a specific space (to sit for meditation near to a shrine) without thinking of anything except the Lord is Bhakti. Limiting your mind to a certain period of time, i.e., from now until the next half hour, repeating the holy name of Krishna is Bhakti. Locking down the mind on the object or on the qualities (of the Lord) and imagining in the Lotus of my heart the luminous, loving form of the Lord is Bhakti. And, when the mind is instructed to focus on a specific object or quality of God [Vastu] for a predetermined amount of time in God [Desha] in a space with God [Kala], that is the true essence of Bhakti-yoga: to have all in one and all in one. This is what Bhakti-yoga is all about.

The Way of Knowledge

V

Introspection

"He who cries in pain will wait for happiness to smile; he who smiles at the pain stays blissful all the while...!"

Avyuth is in his mid-40s, an exponential business person who has preluded his entirety and success within the frame of wealth and riches. He has an outstanding family of four members, including his wife, a son, and an elderly daughter. He serves all his relationships in harmony and happiness. For the last 15 years, he has maintained his accuracy as a family man and with his wife; as a father, he demonstrates that he is a great father; and as a social person, he acts as n expert.So far, he has served as a great pick to play his bat across the pitch of life quite comfortably.

On a certain day, while he was working as a boss in his office, he received a call from an unknown number. The call told him that he would die in the next 24 hours and his company was going to do away with everything very soon. He hung up the phone, thinking it was a prank by one of his amusing friends, and he didn't pay much attention to it after that.Five minutes later, he looked back at the wall clock, and this time, it showed him 10.05, and the time was tickling bit by bit... second by second. With every second passing, it disturbed his mind, and soon it took away the amity of stability and the state of his peacefulness. He had suddenly begun to believe in his agony of death and attempted to call back at the same number, pleading for relief from his impassions and distress.He called his wife to check if she was right and asked her about the children. He had only dropped them back at the school on the way to the office, which he had forgotten. He looked at the clock, and this time it was at 10.15 AM. After a while, one of his employees entered his cabin and told him that the ongoing deal with the previous client had been cancelled for no reason. This very news shook him all at once, and he could not believe in his ears that the company was now on the verge of an end without the investment of their prime investors. By the end of the day, almost all of the investors had sold their shares in the company, leaving him with the darkest back of everything he had built over the previous 25 years.The situation worsens when some investors ask him to give back the money that he has invested in the market to gain a profit. They even claimed to sue his property and all the belongings he has acquired over the years of challenging work and profit. He looked at the clock, and it was 7 in the evening. All the employees and office staff have left him alone in the office with the hope of not returning. He removed the suit from his shoulder and walked out of the office, permanently revealing that the company no longer exists; he is neither a boss nor a wealthy man.All he thinks is that he can't buy any more lists of happiness for his family, no more diamond necklaces for his wife, no more expensive gifts for his children, nor would there be any more stardom left for him in society without the power of money. While contemplating the world's material exclamations, he forgets to smile for the fact that his breath is still present and flowing for his survival.Instead, he regrets the act of his own life, which has left him without the power of riches and wealth; as a result, he has decided to cut off his life and respond to death as the only option left.He jumped off the bridge.

The alarm clock snoozed at 6 in the morning, and he jumped off the bed with a surprise: Am I still alive? Oh, no!Yes, I am alive. Here I am. Nothing has happened to me. And here are my wife and kids.

Nothing has happened to them. And what about my company? It's still there. There is nothing that happened anywhere; it was all just a dream... a bad dream.

A dream is nothing but a reflection of our mind, craving for various thoughts in the world, with the only reality being our presence in it. As long as it is invested in the song of God, you and I will become a true expression of his love and lifelong happiness at all times.

VI

Not A Thing, Not Nothing

In the world of so many wonders and happenings, we have all been seated at the edge of exploring life into many different sects. The glory of our past karma, irrespective of whether it is too good or too bad, has brought us forth to the world of "Samsara" to rejuvenate our ancient past and withstand the world present before us today. All of us, knowingly or unknowingly, desire to fulfil this glory of life in order to find a way out of the cycle of birth and death and to achieve the ultimate epitome of blissfulness, "Nirvana" or "Moksha," which Advaita Vedanta has declared for more than 14000 years.

In India, philosophical enquiry and spiritual enquiry are not two different things. The word for philosophy in India is "Darshana," which literally means "seeing into reality." So, whether we call it "philosophical inquiry" or "spiritual inquiry," it will lead us to spiritual knowledge and get rid of ignorance.

Philosophical enquiry is important for gaining spiritual illumination. One should engage oneself in spiritual pursuits to acquire spiritual knowledge that will eventually set one free. Why is philosophical enquiry important? Except for philosophical inquiry, no other source of knowledge produces knowledge [Vichara]. Just as we cannot see anything without turning on the light in the darkness. Beneath the language of love, there lies faith in the self-effulgent light.

The path of knowledge does not mean reading a lot of books or attending a lot of lectures. It also does not mean sitting in some meditation posture and scratching your back or any of that. The path of knowledge is "Atma-Vichara," an inquiry into the self. It is not about knowing many things but knowing one; it is not about having many ideas but knowing who/what I am.

"Happiness" is the ultimate goal of human life, and none can deny the fact that everyone in the pursuit of happiness is deeply sad sometimes. Surprisingly, unhappiness is because we crave happiness at the time. Now! If our goal in life is to be happy, what is the harm in chasing it all the time? To understand this secret fact of life, we have to passionately wait and imbibe a moment of deep silence to take a journey towards the way within.

Many people often think that philosophical inquiry is something academic and spiritual pursuits are something spiritual. On this, Swami Vivekananda says, "The whole purpose of religion is to manifest the divinity within." Do it by worshipping a God; do it by navigating the mind in meditation; do it by acquiring knowledge about the self; do it by unselfish service... or all of this. '

Now one of you may ask, "Can action exist without desire?" And the monks would answer, "Yes, it is!" But again, we need to understand that there is a difference between action with selfish desire and action with unselfish desire. An action without desire here would mean an action without selfish desire. The desire for the welfare of humanity is an altruistic desire, so it would not be considered harmful, yet that would not be included in the category of desires. In Sanskrit, the term that is used for desire is "Kama". "Kama" is usually a selfish desire, and "Nishkama" would be without selfish desire.

Swami Vivekananda first started his organisational work in the West. His Vedantic teachings are classified into four yogas, namely: Raja yoga, Karma yoga, Bhakti yoga, and Jnana Yoga. While reflecting upon the speciality of why we should read Swami Vivekananda, we would find that Swami Vivekananda has restated in the modern context the ancient teachings of Vedanta. He gave new ideas about the old teachings and a new way to look at the voice of Vedanta philosophy. Swami Vivekananda was very much acquainted with both the developments in science and philosophy in his golden times. He was a unique synthesis of east and west, indeed a man of the entire world.

Like his spiritual master, Sri Ramakrishna Paramhamsa, he too was a teacher of harmony. His spiritual intention was to establish harmony between the world's different religions. He told people that there should be a balance between religion and reason in the different ways to live a spiritual life, from knowledge (Jnana-yoga) to devotion (Bhakti-yoga) to meditation (Raja-yoga) to service (Karma-yoga).

Swami Vivekananda points this out bravely; he states, "Everybody dies." Saints die, and sinners die. Kings die, and beggars die. The learner dies, and the ignorant die too... everybody shall die.' In "A Brief History of Thought: A Philosophical Guide to Living", the French philosopher Luc Ferry wrote that philosophy is not critical thinking about the issues of interest or thinking about critical thought. Instead, philosophy is to grapple with the problem of death. Ernst Becker's classic book "The Denial of Death" says that everyone has a deep-seated fear of death but that this fear is doomed to fail one day because we are all going to die.

Modern psychology is talking about a phenomenon called "the hedonist trap" where it claims that the expectation of happiness that we have [before buying a gadget] and the actual experience that we get [after buying a gadget] is much less than what we expected. The expectation of happiness is what makes us do things that nature wants us to do. Nature wants us to pass on the basics of eating, sleeping, and having children so we can continue to live by making us want pleasure and happiness.

Robert Wright, who is an atheist and a neo-Darwinist, says in his books that "spirituality helps us put our ideas into action. Everything in the world is a master of suspicion, where religion is falsified, philosophy encircles itself and never gets anywhere, and science simply reveals that we are perishable material beings that last for a few years. Therefore, there is no real answer to happiness or unhappiness. I criticise everything and find everything so critical.'

Albert Camus in "The Myth of Sisyphus" begins by saying, "All great deeds and all great thoughts have a ridiculous beginning. Great works are frequently born on a street corner or in a restaurant's revolving door.'

Upon interviewing Richard Dawkins, he was asked to justify his inclination towards atheism when only a tiny percentage of human beings are atheists and believe in some or other religion. A poll was done of living Nobel Prize winners, and more than 90% of them no longer believe in God. So now I leave it to you to conclude. The smarter you are, the less likely you are to believe in religion, and the dumber you are, the more likely you will believe in religion. '

But the greatest answer provided by Swami Vivekananda about the possibility of real spirituality starts here onwards. In the quest to know our real nature as humans, we require these four yogas to become free of bondage. The bondage of life and death, the bondage of seeking and suffering, the bondage of happiness and misery. The purpose of spirituality is to correct the error of ignorance and bring us back to the higher knowledge—"Aham Brahmasmi." As per the highest teachings of spirituality, the root cause of any suffering is highlighted in the ignorance of it being unknown. And the only way to get rid of all pain is to know the truth about yourself.

In the absence of light, one may perceive a rope as a snake. But the slightest beam of light reveals the truth that it was rope alone all the way throughout. The knowledge of the rope radiated through the light, thus putting an end to our ignorance of the rope, which we had seen as a snake.

The path of knowledge gives rise to the path of action. The path of action leads us to the path of devotion, and from the path of devotion, one may head towards the path of meditation, which is to experience and actualize the self from within. All of these different paths lead to the same place, which is "Advaita," which means "not two" which includes :

STAGE ONE :

Let us assume I have a fountain pen in my hand. So the pen is in my hand and I am assuming that you can all see it. Are you? Here is a pen, and I'm holding it up in my hand, and this is quite visible to us one and alike. You are seeing the pen, and so am I. Now, both you and I are the seers, and the pen is seen. Having stated that, it is clear that the two of us are different from each other; we and the pen are hence two different entities. But because we are seeing the pen through an instrument called the eyes, the eyes are the seer and the pen is the seen. Agreed? Very easily, we can identify that the pen is something that is being seen by the eyes alone, and the pen and the eyes are different from each other. See, the same pair of eyes can see many different things. You can see the pen, you can see a notebook right beside me, you can see my palm, and so many other things, but with the same instrument-eyes. So the seen are/can be many, and the seer is but one all the time... our eyes. Also, notice that the sights change all the time. You saw so many things just a little while ago, and now you're sitting and watching something else entirely. So the sight continuously changes, but it is the same eyes. The seer who sees everything as the same and unchanging. The seer is one, and the seen are many. The seer is relatively unchanging, and the seen is always changing.

STAGE TWO:

Let's go even deeper into the concept of the seer and the seen. So the form is seen and the eyes are the seer. (To see from eyes is seeing; to see from the ear is haring; to see from the nose is smalling; to see from te tongue is tasting and to see from the skin is sensing or feeling). It could be a sound, and it is heard by the ears. In this case, the ears are the seers and the sound is the seen, and likewise, it applies to all the senses. Coming back to the theory, the eyes are the seers and the pen is being seen, hence it is the seen object. Now, look closely at whether or not you are wearing eyewear to see an object clearly. How do you know? Because the eyes can't see themselves as they see the pen, objectively. Don't say that you can see your eyes in the mirror. Even that, too, is a reflection of your eyes. So the eyes themselves are being experienced or seen by some other entity. Is it not? If I say, "my eyes are open," who knows about that? My eyes have poor vision and I need to wear glasses. Who directs us to that? Do we ever ask that question, even to ourselves...? I did not... until I saw the truth.

The conditions of the eyes are experienced by the mind. The mind is the seer of our own eyes. That means the mind knows about the eyes, which was the seer seeing the pen in my hand. So, the mind now becomes the seer, and the eyes are seen. "Seer" does not mean actually seeing it physically, but means knowing or being aware of it internally. Here, the mind is the seer or the knower, and the eyes are the seer or known. Again, the seer and the seen must be two different phenomena. The seer is one, and the seen are many. The same mind can know so many things, not just the eyes. The seer is unchanging, and the seen changes continuously.

STAGE THREE :

Now, the same mind that looked unchanging in the beginning is continuously changing into more and more thoughts. The predominant thought brings in more subtle thoughts and becomes an object of sight, witnessed by the intellect. All that was seen by the mind earlier has now been seen by the subtler part of the mind itself. We can call it "consciousness." Here, the mind itself is seen. You can rightly identify when you're feeling happy or miserable. The conditions of your mind are very well understood and witnessed. Once you know the conditions of your mind and the thoughts arising and bubbling in it, then you are surely the knower of the mind. As we have already seen, the seer and the seen must be two different entities. Therefore, it is true that you are surely not your mind, but of course, the mind regulates, in and through you, the consciousness. So, if the mind is the known or seen object, then you are the seer and the mind is the seen. Remember that a seer and seeing are not the same thing. So you are not the mind, but rather the knower of your mind.

STAGE FOUR:

As a result of this, we can conclude that you must be something other than your mind. you are the "witness" or "seer" of your mind. You are the witness of your own mind, and the mind is continuously changing with every new thought. But you, the "witness," are the same and ever unchanging. The witness may see a happy mind or it may see an unhappy mind too. It sees the knowledgeable mind and it sees the ignorant mind as well... and all of them are lit up, revealed by the same seer, you, the witness, which cannot be further witnessed by any external forces. The "witness," which is our real self, can't be objectified and, by its very definition, never becomes an object to be observed, so there is no question of a change in it. The "witness" is beyond any further bifurcation or changes. This unchanging, unshakable witness is the nature of "consciousness," because it is aware of everything and nothing can be aware of itself. Thus, it reveals the mind to your intellect, and through the mind, it reveals the body and the sense organs. Through the body and sense organs, it reveals the entire world, so it is clearly the one unchanging 'existence-consciousness-bliss'"SAT-CHIT-ANANDA".

"While searching for self, I found only evanescent changing thoughts, perceptions, ideas, and memories," writes the great Western philosopher David Hume.I did not find any self anywhere, or where is it? ' But long before David Hume asked, the answer had already been given. People do not see themselves because they do not exist, but because they are not objects that can be seen with physical eyes.The "self" is never an object. Unfortunately, Mr. Hume could not see it anywhere outside and jumped to the conclusion that because there is no evidence of such a self that can be seen by the eyes, therefore the self does not exist. If so, it is true, then who is this person, Mr. Hume, asking for a piece of evidence about himself? Is he not that "self" whom he wants to see outside himself?

Think carefully... and you will realise what spirituality is saying to all of us.Except for you, all the objects, everything we know in life is purely an object.You are not an object, as the entire world is for the self, and that very "self" is your real existence.

Plato famously said in his extensive work of philosophy, "To know the good, one must be good." Aside from his words, the wisdom in truth, most of us could not reconcile the concept of being good.We have contradictions between our hearts and our heads just because our desires are not purified. For him who walks on the path of knowledge, it is love (for God) alone that purifies the soul and heart. Devotion to God (Bhakti Yoga) turns the desires that are flowing towards the world around us back to the feet of God so that they are no longer an obstruction to the path of jnana. Sri Ramakrishna Paramahamsa said it so: "the child who tries to walk holding the hand of the father may slip and fall, but if the father holds your hand, then it is unlikely to slip or fall." Taking refuge in God in this so-called materialistic world is like the eternal father holding your hand and, therefore, there would be no fall.

In the great Asthavakta Gita, it directly says: "If you can see yourself separate from the body-mind complexity and rest in pure awareness (consciousness), you will be peaceful and blissful right now, right at this moment, and become free of all bondage."

True spirituality would ask us to open our sensory eyes to see the world and notice that what we see outside is different from what we see in them. Regard the eyes and notice that the mind is different from the eyes. Regard the mind and notice that the mind is different from "you," the witnessing consciousness. From the world to the mind, all must be present, and even the intellect, which is thinking all these things, too, is sighted by "you" as mere objects. Thus, it says, "You are the eye of the eye, the mind of the mind, and the witness of the intellect, Sakshi [THAT THOU ART]

Just like any other object, the movements of the mind are also known as thoughts, feelings, emotions, etc. I observed the mind and beyond the mind, and that which is beyond the mind is blankness. The experiencer of the mind's movements is that which exists beyond the blankness.Catch it! You are it!

The mind is being seen, but what or what is seeing them cannot be the mind because seer and seeing are not the same thing.Moreover, we can say that the one who is seeing the mind is that it must be consciousness because it is aware after all. So that conscious witness of the mind is called a "Sakshi" witness (as discussed in stage 3).

The ultimate seer is never seen. When the eyes are the seer and the object is seen, but when the eyes themselves are seen by the mind, the mind becomes the object, and so as the mind itself becomes an object of seeing, seen by "Sakshi," the witness, but never becomes seen. It is the ultimate seer. It is the real seer. Now, consider whether you are the Seer or the Seen.Subject or Object?The subject So, if you are Sakshi, and Sakshi is the ultimate seer, the ultimate subject, you will never become a subject of knowledge.

Swami Vivekananda, in his Jnana Yoga lectures, says that "the self is never the object of knowledge." It is always the knower and never the known. But you must not leave with the impression that it is unknown; rather, it is more than known; first, the self is known, and then only everything else is known through that.

The self, or the witness, or the seer, never becomes the seen. It means you are never an object. You are always the subject, the real you, but keep in mind that the real you is not a body. The body is an object, just like the senses are an object, and the mind is an object too. The witness of the mind that senses the body is not an object. The witness is the real YOU! Therefore, if you can honestly, clearly, and with clarity say you are that, then that would be the first step forward towards enlightenment (knowing the self).

Ask yourself why the monks call it a "witness." Because it witnesses the mind, and through that, it witnesses the body, and through the body and mind, it witnesses the world. Do ask why they are calling it "consciousness." Because it gives you a conscious first-person subjective experience. Without it, everything would be blank. Isn't it as simple as that? Ask yourself.

Suppose we close our eyes and now we are unable to see anyone anymore, but we know that we are there. Suppose you put an end to all your thoughts, actions, and desires and stopped thinking. The mind immediately goes blank, but you are still there now, experiencing the deep blank of the mind. Ain't you? That implies, of course, that you are present.So, whether you can see, hear, taste, or touch the world or not, you are the witness of seeing... not seeing, hearing... not hearing, tasting... not tasting, doing... not tasting.But all of that appears to you; you are there all the time, every moment. All the movements of the senses appear to you; you are there all the time. If the senses do not work, you will not be able to see, but you are there. If the mind stops thinking, then you will not be able to know anything, think anything, or even feel anything, but you will be aware of the blank mind. There is a certain blankness, an absence of activity going on that you are aware of all the time. Even if your thinking stops, awareness goes on and on. Thus, in the light of jnana-yoga, if one can see the self as separate from the body, one can rest in nature as pure awareness.

Unlike the yogis of otherness, true knowledge would always ask you to open your eyes, to see the world, and to notice that what you are seeing is different from what you see with your own eyes.It would urge you to regard the eyes and notice that the mind is different from the eyes; it would remind the mind to notice that the mind is different from the witnessing consciousness... you! However, the world must be present, eyes must be present, and the mind must remain active, thinking about all that is going on and ongoing. Even the very intellect that's thinking these things has also become an object of your awareness. Are you not aware that the intellect is thinking these things and that thing? Ask yourself...

That one, who is the witness of the intellect, is you. The witness of the "I" consciousness is you, says Adi Shankarachriya in his hymns.

As we grow from babyhood to childhood to teenage to youth to middle-aged to old age our body changes so much that we could not reclaim it to be the same as it was any longer. The body then becomes an object under your primal awareness and you are aware of it. If the body is an object to our consciousness and we are the subject 'Witness-Consciousness' (as we would know) then we certainly are not the body. It must be different from you. 'I am aware of this body so I cannot be this body'....says the monk.

Let us explore this subtle truth with a story. Robin is a young surgeon, and he writes about his experience of how he discovered the body was a mere casket where a soul takes refuge. He says, "I'm seeing patients on a daily basis and examining their bodies every day." Of all the bodies that they claimed to know as' I am,' which one is the 'I'? I can see every bit of it inside and outside, and I know all the details of these bodies, which I've skillfully learned in medical school, but where does this "I," the conscious being, reside in any of them? All I could see was bones, blood, and flesh, and nowhere could I see the "I am" objectively as the crocked bones in an x-ray report...!

The difference between sentient and insentient is that the insentient (Jada) can never know the sentient (Chit) because you are aware of it but it is not aware of you. Now intelligent minds may ask a monk: Though a pen (it) could not know me (I/you), what about the person sitting next to me? Is he not aware of me and that I am aware of them?

The monk would reply, "The person sitting next to you is aware of your body, is aware of your behaviour, is aware of your language, but is he aware of your awareness?" Never. Even a great yogi with telepathic abilities will be aware of your thoughts but not of your awareness.Even thoughts are objects too. The only place you sense awareness is yourself, in your own mind. There is nowhere else that you find awareness because everything else is an object to your awareness.

Changing Unchanging-the unchanging experiencer of the changing body, Seer Seen-the unknown knower of the knowing mind, Sentient Insentient-the unexperienced experiencer of the experienced intellect, cannot be the body (Object).

Jnana yoga means "you are aware of the body." That means you are witness-consciousness and what you are aware of (the body) is the object of consciousness. Thus, you are not the body but the knowledge of the body.

❧

All the life forces (prana), i.e., circulation of blood, digestion of food, breathing, all the things that make the body a living body, and that living body is called "Prana" (life). So am I the 'Prana' of life? That sound seems to be more promising and subtler for the physical body. The self is "Prana" — the life.

Now the objections arise: is the "Prana" changing? Yes, it is ever-changing. Sometimes it is healthy, sometimes it is unhealthy; sometimes it is hungry, and sometimes it is full and satiated. Sometimes it is energetic, sometimes tired. Hence, the tides of the 'Prana' life are ever moving in and out of the body. Our health, energy, and vitality are changing all the time. The monk says, "Change and unchange is a constant phenomenon in our consciousness." I was the one who felt sick. Now I am the one who feels quite alright. You cannot say that the sick one is somebody different and now I'm the healthy one who is different from the sick one. You are the one who felt sick and you are the one who felt healthy. That means you have not changed, but the "prana" has changed (from a sick body to a healthy body). Again, the theory of change and unchange arises here. As a result, you are no longer the "Prana," but rather an observer of the changes in the life forces.

According to the philosophy of Vedanta, it says if you are aware of the breath, then you are not the breath. Because the breath is the "Drishya," the seen (object), and you are the "Drastha," the seer (subject). So, you are the awareness of the breath. You are aware of your in-breath and it is you who is aware of your out-breath too. But that "awareness" (you) is unchanged, and thus you are the witness-consciousness. As a result, the awareness must be distinct from what one is aware of. you are awareness.

Are you of sound mind...? From moment to moment, day to day, year to year, so many things and thoughts come and go. Likes and dislikes change, and memories fade away too. Confusion becomes clarity, and clarity becomes confusion once again. From childhood ignorance to youthful days of understanding, a lot has changed in the same mind that you and I are aware of. From memories to forgetfulness, our knowledge is changing. The mind is changing quite continuously. Our remembrances fade away, desires vary, personality transforms, but the "I" within all of us is aware of all of those things. So, in changing and remaining constant, you cannot be the mind.A mind is an object of seeing, and you are the subject (seer) of the mind.

This very intellect, which we are using for understanding the big theories of mathematics, inventions of science, and so on, all of this is being done by the intellect, which is an object of your introspection (awareness). Even the insights of the intellect are lit up by awareness (you). You are awareness-consciousness and the intellect is something that you are conscious of. Thus, you are not the intellect either. If you push beyond that, you'll hit a blank. The blankness, if you are aware of that blankness, then the blankness is an object and you are that which is aware of the blankness, thus different from the blankness, hence you are not the blankness.

By now, you must be aware that whatever you thought you were, you are now NOT those things. Because if you can watch your thoughts, then you are not the thought but the knower of all your thoughts. Certainly so, you are not a thing but you are not no-thing also.

The Greek philosopher Heraclitus said, "You cannot step in the same river twice." This means that the world is constantly changing and that no two situations are exactly the same. Just as water flows in a river, one cannot touch the exact same water twice when one steps into a river. The body is just like that, an ever-changing flow of water where there is no second step that is repeated twice. So, if the body is an unreversible flow, then which one of the physical bodies is you?

Infant Body ⟶ Child Body ⟶ Adult Body ⟶ Old Body

The unreversible flow of the Human Body

Awareness never becomes an object; awareness is ever the subject, and whatever you are aware of is insentient, while only the awareness itself is sentient. It's a very elegant knife, and if you apply it to your experience, you will see that it clearly divides into two parts: the pure subject and everything else, i.e., the objective world. The mind's ability to witness the mind itself is called introspection. But the interesting thing is when the mind is not witnessing the mind. Are you not actually trying to see what's in your mind at that time? Don't you get glimpses of happiness and misery ranging from your existing memory? The mind is working all the time, and the inputs or outputs of the mind are presented to you without any effort and even without trying to see what's in your mind. So is it not that it is being presented to consciousness? Ask yourself. Looking at the mind deliberately is a mental activity, but when we don't do that, even then, the activities of the mind are continuously presented to us. Do you always see something delightful, just like we don't ask our nose when it smells a rose in the garden? Are you delighted, Ms. Nosey? No, because we immediately have a smiley face that reflects our happiness in smelling the sweet rose. So, delightfulness was experienced directly without the mind thinking about it. That which is effortlessly experiencing delight or lack of delight in the mind is called consciousness, which is the reality of our true nature. It is never an object, and none of us as "bodily" entities can ever catch it because it is the one and only thing looking at everything all the time. "Existence-Consciousness-Bliss."

Sister Nivedita once asked Swami Vivekananda, "Is Kali the dream of Shiva?" Vivekananda laughed at it gently, and he said, "Well, we'll have it your way then." The whole universe is the dream of consciousness.

When every night we go to sleep, we continue to exist, but in your dream world. The body is nowhere present in our awareness. And being awake then means when we are stuck in the illusion of the universe with the body. In the Mundaka Upanishad, the definition of being awake reads as "consciousness connected with the sense organs and the physical universe with the body."

The monk says, "There is no problem with being awake in the universe, but being stuck in the universe alone is." Being attached to the red shirt all the time is a problem, but at some times I wear the shirt and pull it off my shoulder, and then there is no problem wearing it again and again, multiple times. The very purpose of the body is to degenerate, which means falling apart continuously from time to time all the time. That's the meaning of the body: "shariram shriyete."

The modern philosopher, David Chalmers, in his theory, "The Hard Problem of Consciousness," says "There is no way in which you can show that the physical body, living brain, and the nervous system produce consciousness." It can be associated with consciousness but can't produce consciousness. The hard problem of consciousness leads us to the idea that consciousness may be a separate thing that uses the brain and nervous system but isn't made by the brain, like a separate person or animal.

Another modern philosopher, Galan Strossen, in his article "The Hard Problem of Matter," says where is the hard problem of consciousness...? Consciousness is directly presented to us all the time. There is no other context except for our awareness, but the real mystery is "matter". The more we investigate "matter" through physics, the more matter is disappearing before us.

From molecules to atoms to subatomic particles to the nucleus to sub-nuclear particles to quarks and now to superstrings...! Where is a matter or what is a matter? That becomes a mystery. He further says, "Consciousness is a mystery because we made it a mystery." He writes: "We have assumed matter is fundamental, the brain is fundamental, and the brain must be producing consciousness, but you can't explain how the brain is producing consciousness, hence it turns into the hard problem of consciousness." However, it's a hard problem only because we have assumed that the brain is producing consciousness and you and I can't explain how. Hence,***'ignorance of anything is always beginningless but it comes to an end when you start knowing something'.***

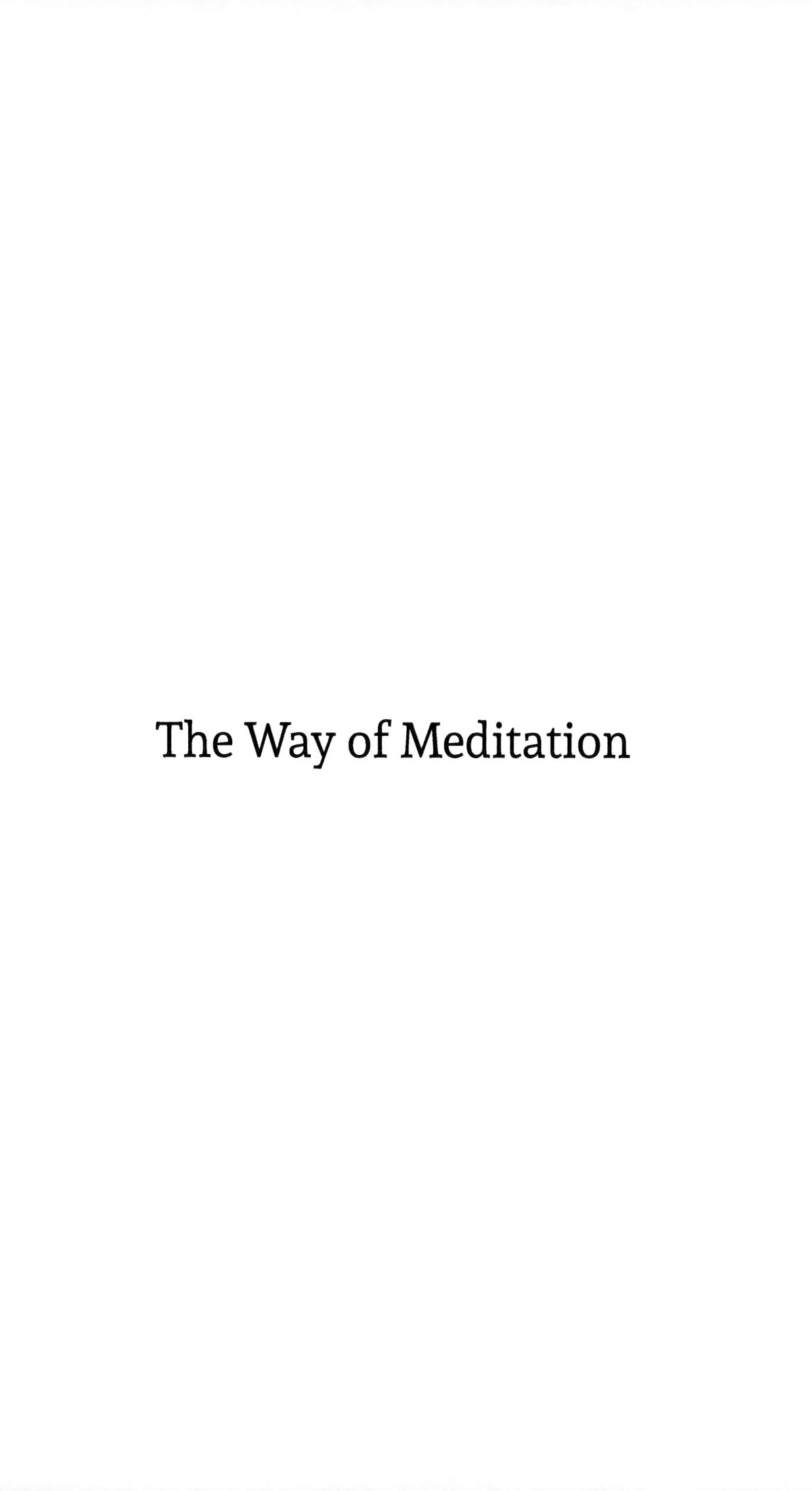

The Way of Meditation

VII

Inculcation

"When you raise your voice in silence, peace is heard all around....!"

It had been raining cats and dogs since the morning. An elderly gentleman, not less than ninety-nine years of age, was resting alone in the corner of his house, witnessing the continuous flux of his thoughts. His thoughts emulated the unstoppable raindrops as if they were absorbed by the earth after heavy rainfall. He had watched the world change for nine long years, from the unknown possibilities to the known impossibilities of so-called experiences that rang with peace and serenity within the sphere of my absolute absurdity.

"Dadu"... I am going to the office! His grandson takes an accord from his father's father and heads towards the school to his workstation. He is tied between the two tiny little hands of his daughter, Ashmi, and son, Aham. His wife, who is standing a few steps ahead of them, is waiting at the door. Therefore, the simple act of bowing down before the old feet looks like a bit of a challenging task for them.

I stayed alone in the glory of his loneliness, chanting and praying the many names of the Lord, God. In the presence of no other-self around, I dwell upon the shortcoming of the sunlight, which does not reach me after a distance of delight. The droplets of the rain played with my old feet like so many wondrous games in which I felt the presence of my son and daughter-in-law, touching below my feet and tickling the time-old tale. Whenever the woof of the wind brushes down my face, I adore the smoothness of my son, kissing my dismantled hands over and over again. When the birds' song reaches my deaf ears, it reveals all the sounds of life above the deafness. The psychedelic colours of the glowing sun reflect a thousand waves of hope, hailing him from the roots of darkness to the temporary light of a few days of my life. The last few drops of the drizzle seem like a blessing. All the seeds that I have thrown into the heart of my awareness have grown into green-less grass that the birds could not pluck and design a dream nest. I have left with a few. He is separating himself from earthly-ness (possessions).

In retrospect, when I wanted to learn more about a single idea I had about the ancient past, it led me through a series of many more ideas. These ideas accumulated, formed, and were registered as so many events (memories). Finally, the asylum for his loneliness sees a great deal of joy and satisfaction in the solitude of my own breath.

When I am awake, I find myself mostly alone, but in the state of a dream, I happened to find myself surrounded by the free will of my thoughts enacted, representing so many things at random, and then when I got into a deep sleep state, I could not even see myself or the truth of my own presence, even in the clear light of glowing darkness. In all of these three states, I have found one commonality of existence that is constantly there all the time. It was there, it is still present here, and it will always be present there even after the world. It is the only thing that remains unchanged in this changing world. It remains untouched by the sensory pains and pleasures of this world, unheard, and yet it is beyond the limits of time and space to encounter the reality of its existence. The limitlessness is there, the "existence" is consciousness, is bliss, and the only reality that existed was 'your own existence'.

ꟸ

VIII

Finite is Infinite, Infinite is Finite

"Peace" is a beautiful gift of nature extracted from the state of consciousness, and the name given in the Upanishads is "Shantam," which means "silent and peaceful." Talking about the very heart of any human being is so peaceful. Still, due to some complexities of life, we think of ourselves as a dilapidated entity with all sorts of myths and misery. In the voice of Adi Shankaracharya, in Vivekachudamani, he says, "Brahma satyamjagatmithya, jivobrahmaivanaparah." Brahman alone is real, the world is the appearance [of Brahman], and there is ultimately no difference between Brahman and Atman, the individual self.

Spirituality is not possible without morality. One must have a calm mind to experience life in reality. The four yogas are part of the path shown by the yogis [self-realised ones] to see the same divinity everywhere and in all beings, living and non-living. That which is within is also outside. That which you discover with eyes closed in the deepest meditation is also exactly what you see with eyes open and engaged with the world. That which you see in the waking world is the same reality that shines forth in the world of dreams. It is the same reality which shines forth but unmanifest in the world of deep sleep.

Swami Vivekananda very famously said, "One only exists; it appears as nature [world] and soul [god]." In his beautiful words, Meister Eckhart writes, "the ground of my soul and the ground of God are the same ground."

All of our thoughts, feelings, emotions, desires, and perceptions are flung around in our minds like a restless monkey, which is restless by nature. Now suppose the monkey-mind drank a glass of wine and, at the same time, a scorpion stung it on the back...? Consider that.So, restlessness. The very fact that one cannot hold on to one thought for any length of time, for a minute or two or five, shows that the mind has impurities, and hence it needs a cure in concentrated meditation.

Our minds run in patterns, and those patterns are not easily altered. Unless someone chooses to work at it, it will remain the same, disturbed and troublesome. When the mind becomes agitated, it is difficult to remain a witness and difficult to avoid suffering in the world, the monks say.

People who have obsessive-compulsive disorder (OCD) often find themselves doing the same thing over and over again, even though they know their mind is interfering with their unrestrained psychological behavior.

As Swami Vivekananda would say, the mind is very difficult to control. But controlling the mind has to be learned with a strong will of concentration and certain psychological practices. So, controlling the monkey mind is the subtlest of all tasks and the greatest of all adventures. So it will take a lot of time and effort to get it to the point where you can meditate on it.

Everything that civilisation gives us is not given directly by nature. The words that we read, the letters that we scribble, the food we eat, and the walks we took in childhood had to be taught.

In ancient Indian philosophy, it is said that"... there is no knowledge higher than knowing about the self; 'Who/what am I?' There is no power greater than the power of systematic repetition, enabling the mind to manifest that knowledge. As a result, insight is the most important thing you can learn, and repetition is the most important thing you can do.

Going beyond worldly desires [dispassion] is essential to practising meditation. Any movement of the mind when it flows towards the outside enchantments, any movement of the mind develops into a desire of "I want...". It can go to the level of an obsession or an addiction that will not allow the intellect [Chitta] to remain centred on its core. Quietly in the distance, a western neurologist, Sigmund Freud, speculated on human behaviour and coined the term "libido" as a basic psychic emotion of worldly urges that constitute human activity and behaviour. He says, "Any movement of the subject [self] to the object [worldly pleasures] is "libido."

As the holy monks say, "neither do you seek for the world to be true, nor should you avoid it being untrue." Rather, be quiet and quietly be in it [meditation] because you are on the journey to enlightenment, beyond the true and untrue. "

Religion is a realisation. Religion is not giving your consent to a set of doctrines, not giving your commitment to something that you have been taught, but actually practising and experiencing something. You know it's real only when you have experienced it. Swamiji Vivekananda. Among the four yogas, the "Raja Yoga" is basically called the path of meditation. The Raja yogi says that it's not a question of believing something, it's a question of experience.

Swamiji Vivekananda, when he visited the western horizons many years ago, used to say, "If somebody says to you that I have seen God but you cannot, and you must follow me, you must believe me." Do not follow such a person. But if somebody says, "I have seen God and you can too," then you can follow such a person. Thus, religion is something to be experienced first. In India, it has been understood for aeons that religion is not ultimately meant for belief because here we have the example of so many saints and monks, generation after generation, who have actually had the vision of

God, irrespective of whatever the tradition is. They have seen God truly and absolutely.

In the cultural folklore, we have the songs sung by Mirabai and many others who have the vision of Lord Krishna as their companion, "Sakha". Old Sabri had glimpses of Lord Rama in his godly divine form. And not only that, but even the thieves saw Rama and Lakshmana protecting the house of the saint Tulsi Das. So, having the vision of God and these mystical experiences are found not only throughout the history of Hinduism but in every religion. At the core of every religion, there are mystics, saints, and monks who claim not only that they believe in something, or that they have understood something, but they have actually seen God in real life. The path of Raja Yoga says that this is our goal, and we must actually experience these realities. For that, there is a method, a set of psychophysical exercises that if you and I practice, we will realise that we will experience the vision of God (the effulgent energy of the universe).

In the paradigm of devotion 'Bhakti-Yoga', it says that God exists. But if you do not have faith in God; if you do not believe in God or if you do not worship or surrender to God then you would not see God and that is the cause of all our suffering and so the solution is faith in God. However, in 'Raja-yoga' the path of meditation, the paradigm is our minds are restless and therefore we do not see the truth. If the minds can be concentrated, focused, calmed then we will see this truth for ourselves. We will experience it. Though we might argue with somebody else's experience, if we experience it to our satisfaction then we are satisfied personally and hence we do not argue with our own experiences. So this is the path of experience ~ Meditation.

In this world of modernity, technological noises, and chaos, we do not experience it right now because our minds are scattered everywhere else. We are neither focused nor concentrated on our inner serenity to procure the sound of silence within us all. To eradicate this outer rush and to bring forth inner concentration, Raja-yoga stood for us with specific methods to focus or concentrate our minds to realise the trueness of our divine self, "Atman."

In Buddhism and Jainism, there are a variety of meditative methods and techniques to calm the mind down to its basic blissful nature (The Mindfulness Meditation). In Hinduism, the 'Patanjali Yoga Sutras, lay their foundation in specializing on the path of meditation.

Besides, meditation is a very popular subject today, but it is also universally acknowledged to be difficult too. There are so many techniques of meditation across different traditions that we may get to see a whole supermarket of techniques available to us. It derives from Buddhistic vipassana meditation, which has since evolved into modern mindfulness meditation.This mindfulness meditation is taught in corporate offices, schools and colleges, jails and rehabilitation centres, and also in the military as well. The Tibetan Buddhists have a variety of sophisticated visualisation techniques. In Hinduism, more precisely in the Vaishnava tradition, the visualisation of the deity called "Dhyana Slokas" teaches us how to visualise the deity upon meditation. Indeed, it is from these traditions that the visual iconography and images of the Gods and Goddesses have evolved over time.

The Russian Orthodox book "The Way of the Pilgrim" talks about practising the Jesus Prayer (the prayer of the heart) in which the devotee has to repeat the prayer (Lord Jesus have mercy upon me...), which is an example of "mantra Japan" in the Hindu tradition. It is basically a "mantra japan" and the devotee, in a very simple way, throughout all the ups and downs of life, goes on repeating the prayer "mantra" and his mind is always on God (Jesus). In Sufism, they have their own meditation techniques to centre their minds on meditation. So meditation, therefore, is a worldwide phenomenon that is to be acknowledged and practised in all circumstances.

In the book, 'Meditation by the Monks of the Ramakrishna Order', in the second essay 'Before You Sit in Meditation,' Swami Ashokananda gives us ten points to the practise of meditation.

First, he asked us to be regular in meditation. That means to meditate daily. Meditation is a practice. There is no good or bad meditation, but to start meditating. If you sit quietly in the morning and evening for at least 10 minutes each, then you've already made a start. He says so.

True meditation has to do with the mind, and the mind is also a body. Just like the physical body, the mind is also a body (Sukshma Sharira), a subtle body that needs to be regulated daily. Remember, we are not the mind, but we have a mind, and spirituality is basically in the mind. The significance of saying the mind is that the mind is a body because the body does not need information, but it needs training. Say, for example, you want a fit body and, in the pursuit of achieving a fit body, you have read all the colourful pages in green and red, so-called articles about healthy food habits, the art of clean eating and exercising, newsfeeds and books... But will the body become fit just by reading all kinds of stuff? I guess not. Maybe it will get a little sicker than before after reading all those books. However, if you exercise every day in the morning, even without reading a single book, your body will begin to show the changes and it will slowly achieve healthiness. Similarly, the mind, being that it is a subtle body, requires training. So, the mind also requires training. Training is repetition. It is neither information nor understanding, but repetition.

In his book "The Happiness Hypothesis," Jonathan Haidt speaks about the zillions of solutions prescribed in so many "good" books as information available for the readers to read, follow, and practice. But if those books did any good for them, then many of our lives would have been transformed. There is so much wisdom, interesting, inspiring stories and techniques were written that promised us to learn "how to win friends and influence people" or "the art of public speaking," written by Dale Carnegie. All of these books and writings, though they are anecdotal and may not be very rigorous, still extend some useful and practical advice, and yet why are our lives still miserable? This is a serious question to be asked.

People go ahead and buy so many new self-help books to hanch for happiness in mere scribbles. And then within a few weeks, they would have made many friends and influenced so many people's lives, but why is it that their lives are not changing? Jonathan Haidt takes up this question seriously and says that because we do not understand the model of our personality, our lives continue to stay miserable. He gives the example of the elephant and the rider, saying that the rider knows exactly where he wants the elephant to go. He can read a map and decide to move towards a certain direction, but he has no strength to make the elephant go there unless the elephant agrees to go because their elephant is much stronger than the rider himself. He can only guide the elephant, but if the elephant wants to go in the opposite direction into the banana forest, then the rider cannot do anything besides be helpless. Just like that, our intellect, "Buddhi," is like an elephant rider, and the body, "Deha," is like an elephant. Much like the elephant, our body does not respond to lectures, seminars, papers, or TED talks...! It is the intellect that pushes the mind to act upon the subject, along with the body. Now let me ask: what does the elephant respond to information or training? Training is not it? Unlike bodies, elephants are wild creatures, so they are trained to respond to certain commands. Similarly, making any kind of training habitual requires repetition and time. It's not enough to listen to something and understand it immediately without continuous, rigorous training. The body can be trained to get up at 4 o'clock in the morning and make it easy and effortlessly.

According to Haidt, the gut and certain other parts of the body almost have an autonomous intelligence. It has bunches of nerves to operate digestion automatically in the body (stomach) and so they have a kind of inner decision-making ability regarding food and other sense pleasures that might override your intellect and might exert a pull, so you have to be trained to consume good habits first.

Second, Swami Ashokanandaji recommends we have a fixed time for meditation at least twice a day, both in the morning and evening. The best time to practise meditation is upon waking up in the morning. It is always good to get up early from bed, biding the previous day's impressions good bye. Use that time for meditation when the world is quiet.

There are so many beautiful instances of Swami Vivekanand in New York. He would always be in a meditative mood, and sometimes he would sit quietly and become so absorbed in the deep quietness of his heart for hours and hours. Like many of his, the reminiscences describe how the evening fell upon the city (Manhattan) as the night deepened in the sky; Swami Vivekananda would remain immersed in Samadhi (meditative mood) in his little room. Being the diving soul that he is, he would try to keep his mind from entering deep meditation at all hours; quite the opposite of us, who tried and failed to enter deep meditation even once.

In India, the yogis felt that there are certain times in the day when the night changes into the morning (from dusk to dawn) in the noontime. There are inflexion points, so to speak. The twilight, when the afternoon changes into the evening, and then midnight, are the good times for meditation. The mind of a monk (yogi) should become like that of a compass in a meditative mood so that whenever the world throws our mind into a spin of problems and difficulties, it always whirls around and it takes effort to bring it back to that axis pointing towards God-realization.

Third, Swami Ashokanandaji asked us to have a proper place to sit for meditation. It could either be a corner in your room or the whole house, or one could furnish a special meditation seat for oneself too. There are auspicious places like temples, mosques, churches, meditation halls, interfaith rooms, etc., where people have thought about God or contemplated quietly for a long time, which have holy vibrations and make them perfectly suitable for practising meditation. Finding ourselves in the right place at the right time is a big support to our minds, and people do feel a deep sense of celestial vibration (A-U-M) intuned with them all the time.

Regularity, time and place are therefore associated with calmness, peace and serenity.

The difference between a worldly mind and the mind of the meditator (yogic mind) [the one who meditates and the one who does not meditate] is that the non-yogic mind, non-meditating mind, or worldly mind is like that of a gushing river full of impure thoughts moving and changing fast, and we don't know where it will take us in the end. The worldly mind gives no peace, neither to oneself nor to those who are or will be around. Just like the stale and muddy water, it is unable to quench anyone's thrust. But the yogic mind, or the meditative mind, is like that of a sweet and clean river in winter, where there will be fewer thoughts but they will be controlled and deliberate. You can drink this water. You can give it to others too. Similarly, the yogic mind stays at peace and spreads peacefulness to all. The yogic mind is so clear and peaceful that one can see through to what lies underneath. The mind is but a deep sound of ultimate silence [the "Atman" is beyond the mind- Yoga Sutra].

The moment a person sits for meditation, he/she/they will attract some habitual patterns of thinking, which many times we may call negative or impure thoughts. Those thoughts were always there, but we're not aware of them until we encash some inner calmness. We never paid an eye to seeking through our basic thoughts, but when the mind is quietened in meditation or we sit quietly, sometimes these thoughts become vivid in our conscious experience, emulating our unconscious world of thoughts and desires. It is just like if you ever try to dry out an ink pen from the ink pot by the tip of your fingers, at first it will shred more and more dark ink before bringing out the crystallised ink for a clean, clear, and better handwriting. Likewise, in meditation, first the negative thoughts will come out, but when you observe them quietly without getting carried away or feeling disturbed by those thoughts, you'll experience something different, something peaceful and fulfilling within the self itself. Thoughts are mere dirt, and accumulated patterns of thought are there in your mind, but they are not the real you! ....They may scare you with all those depressing thoughts or negative thoughts, violent thoughts, resentful thoughts, etc. But if you don't give in to it and just watch the thoughts carefully, they will go away all on their own. Getting caught up in the thoughts or the web of thoughts is very dangerous, and hence one needs to be aware of the self "Atman" in the delight of meditation [Atmachintan]. However, mentally disturbed or unsteady individuals are thus questioned about sitting for meditation, as it might be dangerous for their minds if they're not strong enough to handle their powerful subtle emotions. For such minds, it is much better to get engaged in some worldly activities to serve socially and declutter their minds through action [Karma-Yoga]. They could be involved in some creative activities or community services to break the chain of unpleasant negative thoughts and patterns to bring in the positiveness in their lives.

One zen way of deep meditation for cleaning up resentful thoughts is the "pebbles in the bubble" technique. With the help of this technique, one may very calmly and steadily cleanse his/her thoughts by putting them into the zen bowl. So there will be two piles of smooth pebbles in white and black. Whenever a disturbing thought comes to mind, take a black stone and put it in the bowl. On the other hand, whenever a pure thought comes and uplifts the mind, take a white pebble and put it in the bowl and watch your mind carefully. In the beginning, we may perceive that the bowl is mostly filled with black stones and only a few white pebbles in between, but within a few weeks of mindful practice, more white pebbles will accumulate in the bowl than the lesser black ones. As the mind calms down, it becomes more [Sattvic] pure, pious, and precious.

Fifth, Swami Ashokanandaji forbids us to be in a cluster of bad companies. He states, "whose company [bad company] we keep could cause a very powerful impact on your mind." In "bad company," it is not pejorative in the sense that a person is bad or immoral, but in the sense that a person may be very worldly in nature, and if you and I keep company with such a person, knowingly or unknowingly, in the end, it will definitely affect our minds, indulging in iniquitous thoughts. However, one good advantage of practising spiritual disciplines is that such people [bad company] will find you utterly boring and very soon they will move away from your quest for more meaningless fun in the outside world.

Being humans, though we are well aware of our physical strength and its limitations, we are mostly unaware of the strengths of our own minds or limitations. We can run a 100-meter race but may not be able to swim across the English Channel in 30 minutes; we can lift a pair of 50-pound dumbbells in the gym, but we may not be able to lift 200 pounds that easily. Just like physical strength, even our mental mind has its own capacity, which takes a rigorous amount of training and continuous practice.

Over the many years of ignorance, our mind has become so used to all kinds of worldly thoughts, desirous thoughts, envious thoughts, angry thoughts, resentful thoughts, and so on. These are to do with the world, and when we sit for meditation with this baggage of thoughts and desires, shall we be able to experience calmness in the mind? Because of the bad patterns of thinking habits influenced by a bad company, it brings out the tendencies that are mostly delirious and evil. On the contrary, coming into contact with the holy company brings out all of our delirious thoughts, compiling the habit of positive thinking.

So we must be careful of the company we keep. A good company is good, but if you don't get a good company, then no company is a better company to be with. As Guru Rabindranath Tagore sings loudly in Bengali - [যদি তোর ডাক শুনে কেউ না আসে তবে একলা চলো রে।] If no one responds to your call, walk on your own (alone).Only the ignorant man [Agnani] is terrified by the thought of solitude and laments over the fact that "Alas I am alone!". But the learned ones [Gnani]—knowers of the Atman—say that solitude is the highest state of happiness for [him/her/them].The very definition of "Moksha" in the Yoga Sutras is "aloneness" [Kaivalya]. Plotinus says—"Spirituality is the journey of the alone to the alone." So solitude is not lonely, but rather great bliss.Whereas the ignorant person is lonely, the spiritual person enjoys solitude [one's own company] to the fullest. Satsanga [holy company] is the vessel that transports us across the ocean of samsara [world life].

The sixth point that Swami Ashokanandaji advised us on is asceticism [Tapasya]. Asceticism means living in austerity. Asceticism in Vedanta is called "Titiksa". A chunk of good sleep, comfortable living, worldly enjoyment, delicious food [non-sattvic], irrelevant company and entertainment to make do a little less of it is called "Tapasya"... asceticism. "Wherever the mind relaxes and tries to let go or left loose, just tighten it up a little bit..."-says the Swami. The main purpose of asceticism is to make the mind concentrated and powerful so that one can think of God without much difficulty. Our mind and body come under the control of intelligence [Buddhi], but we must also be careful if we deprive it too much and too fast. The mind will keep thinking about what you have deprived it of. One way of practising asceticism is to deal with the troubles of life. Despite a little illness, I will still meditate. Beyond the troubles in life, I will pursue my spiritual disciplines, which is a good way of practising asceticism. Putting up with the sorrows of the world because of love for God is what the monks do in asceticism.

Seven, to feel completely detached from all the roles of "I" as father, mother, son, daughter, friend, foe, boss, millionaire! And stop giving themselves all the importance in the world because 'nothing in the world depends on you... nothing in the world depends on us'. Swami Ashokanandaji speaks of it beautifully when he says, approaching God with the sense of eternity.

Any good or bad day in our lives, no matter how joyful or scandalous, will pass away in the wind of time, and when we look back on our thoughts, say 30 years later, it will become a small thing in our memory that will mostly be forgotten after so many years... why do we give happiness and sadness so much importance even now, as it should not have been given that day?

Martin Luther, the founder of the protestant movement, speaks nicely when he says, "every day I spend an hour on my knees praying to God, and when I have no time at all [excessive work], I spend two hours on my knees praying to God."

The monks say, "Come to God with a feeling of eternity; detach from everything only "I and now my Lord and nothing else and that is the truth."

Every night at midnight, when you go to sleep, you are relieved of all your responsibilities.is no father, mother, husband, wife, rich or poor. There is not even a single assurance in our lives that we will wake up tomorrow when there are eighty thousand ways to die in a single day! Why do we give ourselves so much self-importance?

Eight, he says, yearning for God is critical for those seeking the path of spirituality.Do I want it? is the big question to ask first. Swami Ashokanandaji asked us to simulate the idea of actually knowing the height and imagine the intense desire to see God in his most divine form. Just like Sri Ramakrishna sees the divinity in the form of mother Kali, or the intense seeking of Swami Vivekananda seeing the vision of God.

In all the lives of the great saints and monks, men and women, mediaeval or modern, there is one thing that they all had in common: their intense hunger to seek God. If there is a strong desire to seek anything, then everything we do is to get that one thing we so desire [be it God or not God!]. Whatever we want in life, we arrange everything accordingly and try to get it alone. It is only when we do not want [God] that we engage in a plethora of techniques, methods, books, and so on in order to obtain God.

According to Sri Ramakrishna, a very thirsty man will remove the scum on the top and try to sip the water from the puddle on the ground, whereas a person who is not thirsty will never even consider drinking the water from the mud.

Nine, Swami Ashokanandaji says, has an inseparable connection with the divine throughout the day. Have an eternal emotion [bhava] for meditation throughout the day. One should not jump into meditation without emotion towards God. According to monks, the best way to practise meditation is to sit quietly for some time, quiet the mind, and then gently enter into deep meditation. After you have finished, sit quietly for some time before you come back into the world of sounds.

As Sri Ramakrishna says, "be awake in yoga and yaga". "Yoga" means association, visualization, connection, meditation in the name of God, and "Yaga" means service and sacrifice. So connect yourself to God throughout the day somehow or other.

Finally, according to Ashokanandaji, the most important thing for progressing along the Raja Yoga [meditation] path is to find the company of the holy [Satsanga]."Once you meet such a person [holy company], the reality of spiritual life cannot be denied; once you see such a person [holy company], even briefly, you will never forget it for the rest of your life," he said.The more you see such a person, the more your life changes a deep impression, and you will realise at the end of your life that it was the most valuable part of your life to meet those people. This is the power of the holy company. Swami Ashokanandaji further writes, "If such a person tells you God is real and you are not the body, not the mind, then run away." You have an immortal soul; it convinces you at a very profound level, and you will feel convinced.

In the other paradigms, yoga or spirituality means joining the "Jeevatman" to the "Paramatman" (the sentient beings to the supreme self), but in Raja-yoga, "Yoga" certainly means separation and not joining with the world [outside]. The whole problem of dissatisfaction in the world is that we have become bound to material nature. Say the monks say, "you are spirit but you have become joined to a material nature... you are consciousness but you have become mixed up with matter and that is worldliness [samsara], the beginning of all the problems. Therefore, the whole purpose of yoga is to separate consciousness [Purusha] and matter [Prakriti] to show us that we are not material but pure spirit. According to Patanjali's Yoga Sutra, yoga is the cessation of the modification of the mind, "Chitta Vritti Nirodhaha". So the purpose of yoga is to calm the mind down and make the mind one-pointed so that there is no turbulence in the mind.

If spirituality and materiality exist in the realm of illusion [Maya], then what is spirituality actually? It is shifting the reference of the "I" [Mind, Intellect, Ego] from worldliness to oneness [from body-mind back to consciousness] and what the modern materialists speak about materialism is that consciousness may "somehow" originate in a physical body from the living brain.

In his book, Allan Watts defines the idea of "consciousness" in the form of a simple children's tale that tells how God [consciousness] pretending to be not-God [worldliness] has totally forgotten that he is God himself. He then goes around searching for himself in the world. This search for his own real nature gave birth to the world of illusion [Maya/Samsara]. From the worst of sufferings to the greatest of achievements, life seems to be a continuous play in the desert, looking for water in the mirage.

On what does your freedom depend? Does it depend upon calming the mind, which is a product of the world, or putting the mind into a quick online'sahaj samadhi programme', which could equally be a trick of the mind that gives you freedom? If that gives you freedom, then perhaps you will never be free of the mind and keep on buying this "one-hour happiness" online. Decide for yourself. The real freedom is in knowing the self as "consciousness" is ever free of all the bondage of pain and pleasure, of love and unlove, of birth and death.

According to an old Sankyan storey about "consciousness" and "nature," The storey goes like this: there is a blind man who cannot see, and there is a lame man who cannot go anywhere. So what do they do? The blind man joins hands with the lame man and puts him on his shoulders. The lame man tells the blind man where to go and what he is seeing in the world. Thus, the blind man carries the lame man on his shoulders wherever he wants to go. This blind man is material nature, and the lame man is consciousness. Consciousness cannot do anything physical or mental by itself, but everything can be experienced only by consciousness. Whereas matter [time-space-energy] can do everything, it can't experience anything without consciousness.

Now, let us analyse this old Sankyan storey using our most common sense. All our experiences, whatever you and I have done in life, or whatever anybody can do and experience in life, have this common structure: subject and object. Upon investigating the "object," we will find nature, and if you investigate the "subject," we will find that at the back of all our objective experiences there lies a subjective consciousness. This is the basic idea behind our real nature: that we are nothing but the same consciousness present in all the forms of the universe.

Swami Vivekananda says that true spirituality is possible only when the lake water [mind] is absolutely clear as crystal and all the waves, bubbles, and ripples have seized into one shining calmness, meeting the surface of silence.

The Final Take Away

Bhagavad Gita - Chapter 2 - Verse 47

"कर्मण्येवाधिकारस्ते मा फलेषु कदाचन। मा कर्मफलहेतुर्भूर्मा ते सङ्गोऽस्त्वकर्मणि॥

Karmanyevadhikaraste-Ma-Phaleshu-Kadachana|Ma-Karmaphalaheturbhurma-Te- Sangostvakarmani"

Sri Bhagawan-Vashya - "You have the right to action alone. You never have the right to the fruit. Do not motivted to act because of the fruit. But don't be motivated to not acting either." **[The above-mentioned translation was taken from Dr. Bibek Debroy's Unabridged version of the Bhagavad Gita. *Debroy, Bibek. The Bhagavad Gita. Penguin Books India, 2005.]***

In this verse, the idea of Karma Yoga is said to be true. A man has the right to work but not the results of his labour. It means that labour should be done with the intention of giving the fruits to the Lord. Man should keep his thoughts free of the desire for the fruits of his action at all times and under all conditions. Otherwise, it is difficult to bring the mind to a state of tranquilly and restfulness, and one-pointed attention becomes impossible. When a man thinks about the results of his work, he is filled with anxiety and failure. This denial of failure stalks him like a demon and clouds his mind with difficulties and hazards. As a result, it obstructs the path to unselfish action more towards the selfish desirs [From Nishkama Karma to Sakama Karma]. The guilt of failure and the frustration of defeat have agitated the emotions. Thus, mental energy is lost on unpleasant feelings, and a man's individuality is shattered on the sands of rage and hated. Life gets dreadful. This is the practical experience of every person on the planet. As a result, we might conclude that effort motivated by desire is a disturbing rather than a purifying force in spiritual sadhana. A man will never be able to see the Self until his intellect is cleaned. As a result, nishkama karma is extremely necessary for spiritual realisation.

Allowing the self to get attached to inaction should be the theme of everyone's life. Quite obviously, Lord Krshna conveys the message to us (the holy lessons taught on the battlefield to Arjuna) that people should not be attached to the things they could get (fruits), but to the things they should do (action). Giving up work demonstrates sloth and inactivity (Tamas). It is a denial of spiritual advancement. When one is sleeping, one accomplishes nothing. However, sleep is not the same as self-realization. The barriers and polls are ineffective. As a result, they are not philosophers. As a result, tamas-caused inactivity should be combated with unselfish activity. This helps to remove all types of sloth and weakness, elevating inner peace and tranquilly. Some individuals, under the influence of ignorance, spend their time in the "darkness of nothingness" and misunderstand it as "self-realization." People like this fail in both their worldly and spiritual lives. It is critical that they recognise tamasic inactivity as the primary adversary in spiritual life. They need to get out of inaction (tamas) and start doing selfless actions. The whole exuberance of human civilization is built on the grounds of work and action (doing-ness). No one can survive without work or labour in some capacity or other. Thus, it has been advised by the one omnipotent and omnicient Lord to perform our actions without attachment to their fruits or results, because results are the epiphenomenon that is associated with every work done in this world. Work done with unselfish motives will provide the greatest joy of freedom (Moksha) and liberate us from the loop of infinite desirs of suffering. Therefore, Nishkama karma is said to be the central theme of the Bhagvad-Gita, preached by the lord himself to all humankind.

Swamiji's Commentraty on the Bhagavad Gita - Chapter 2 - Verse 47

Be beyond the common worldly motives. "To work you have the right, but not to the fruits thereof." Man can train himself to know and to practice that, says the Karma-Yogi. When the idea of doing good becomes a part of his very being, then he will not seek for any motive outside. Let us do good because it is good to do good; he who does good work even in order to get to heaven binds himself down, says the Karma-Yogi. Any work that is done with any the least selfish motive, instead of making us free, forges one more chain for our feet.[1]

Bring all light into the world. Light, bring light! Let light come unto every one; the task will not be finished till every one has reached the Lord. Bring light to the poor and bring more light to the rich, for they require it more than the poor. Bring light to the ignorant, and more light to the educated, for the vanities of the education of our time are tremendous! Thus bring light to all and leave the rest unto the Lord, for in the words of the same Lord "To work you have the right and not to the fruits thereof." "Let not your work produce results for you, and at the same time may you never be without work.[2]

By the by, I have made a discovery as to the mental method of really practising what the Gita teaches, of working without an eye to results. I have seen much light on concentration and attention and control of concentration, which if practised will take us out of all anxiety and worry. It is really the science of bottling up our minds whenever we like.[3]

Despair not; remember the Lord says in the Gita, "To work you have the right, but not to the result." Gird up your loins, my boy. I am called by the Lord for this. I have been dragged through a whole life full of crosses and tortures, I have seen the nearest and dearest die, almost of starvation; I have been ridiculed, distrusted, and have suffered for my sympathy for the very men who scoff and scorn. Well, my boy, this is the school of misery, which is also the school for great souls and prophets for the cultivation of sympathy, of patience, and, above all, of an indomitable iron will which quakes not even if the universe be pulverised at our feet.[4]

How hard it is to arrive at this sort of non-attachment! Therefore Krishna shows us the lower ways and methods. The easiest way for everyone is to do [his or her] work and not take the results. It is our desire that binds us. If we take the results of actions, whether good or evil, we will have to bear them. But if we work not for ourselves, but all for the glory of the Lord, the results will take care of themselves. "To work you have the right, but not to the fruits thereof." The soldier works for no results. He does his duty. If defeat comes, it belongs to the general, not to the soldier. We do our duty for love's sake — love for the general, love for the Lord.[5]

Indian writers are not like modern writers who steal ninety percent of their ideas from other authors, while only ten per cent is their own, and they take care to write a preface in which they say, "For these ideas I am responsible". Those great master minds producing momentous results in the hearts of mankind were content to write their books without even putting their names, and to die quietly, leaving the books to posterity. Who knows the writers of our philosophy, who knows the writers of our Purânas? They all pass under the generic name of Vyâsa, and Kapila, and so on. They have been true children of Shri Krishna. They have been true followers of the Gita; they practically carried out the great mandate, "To work you have the right, but not to the fruits thereof.[6]

Krishna did everything but without any attachment; he was in the world, but not of it. "Do all work but without attachment; work for work's sake, never for yourself.[7]

Let me remind you again, "Thou hast the right to work but not to the fruits thereof." Stand firm like a rock. Truth always triumphs.[8]

To work we have the right, but not to the fruits thereof:" Leave the fruits alone. Why care for results? If you wish to help a man, never think what that man's attitude should be towards you. If you want to do a great or a good work, do not trouble to think what the result will be.[9]

This world is not for cowards. Do not try to fly. Look not for success or failure. Join yourself to the perfectly unselfish will and work on. Know that the mind which is born to succeed joins itself to a determined will and perseveres. You have the right to work, but do not become so degenerate as to look for results. Work incessantly, but see something behind the work. Even good deeds can find a man in great bondage. Therefore be not bound by good deeds or by desire for name and fame. Those who know this secret pass beyond this round of birth and death and become immortal.[10]

Though the ideal of work of our Brahmavâdin[1] should always be "कर्मण्यवेाधिकारस्तेमा फलषेु कदाचन" — "To work thou hast the right, but never to the fruits thereof", yet no sincere worker passes out of the field of activity without making himself known and catching at least a few rays of light.[11]

What is your motive? Are you sure that you are not actuated by greed of gold, by thirst for fame or power? Are you really sure that you can stand to your ideals and work on, even if the whole world wants to crush you down? Are you sure you know what you want and will perform your duty, and that alone, even if your life is at stake? Are you sure that you will persevere so long as life endures, so long as there is one pulsation left in the heart? Then you are a real reformer, you are a teacher, a Master, a blessing to mankind. But man is so impatient, so short-sighted! He has not the patience to wait, he has not the power to see. He wants to rule, he wants results immediately. Why? He wants to reap the fruits himself, and does not really care for others. Duty for duty's sake is not what he wants. "To work you have the right, but not to the fruits thereof," says Krishna. Why cling to results? Ours are the duties. Let the fruits take care of themselves. But man has no patience. He takes up any scheme. The larger number of would-be reformers all over the world can be classed under this heading.[12]

Sources & References

1. The Ideal of Karma-Yoga | Swami Vivekananda- https://vivekavani.com/ideal-karma-yoga-swami-vivekananda

2. Vedanta in its Application to Indian Life https://vivekavani.com/vedanta-application-indian-life-vivekananda

3. CLI Dhira Mata – Letters of Swami Vivekananda

https://vivekavani.com/cli-dhira-mata-letters-swami-vivekananda

4. IV Alasinga – Letters of Swami Vivekananda
https://vivekavani.com/iv-alasinga-letters-swami-vivekananda

5. *Krishna – Swami Vivekananda*
https://vivekavani.com/krishna-swami-vivekananda

6. The Work before us –Swami Vivekananda
https://vivekavani.com/work-before-us-swami-vivekananda

7. Saturday, June 29 – Inspired Talks
https://vivekavani.com/saturday-june-29-inspired-talks

8. XXV Alasinga- Letters of Swami Vivekananda
https://vivekavani.com/xxv-alasinga-letters-swami-vivekananda

9. Karma in its Effect on Character – Swami Vivekananda
https://vivekavani.com/karma-effect-character-swami-vivekananda

10. Unselfish Work is True Renunciation- Swami Vivekananda
https://vivekavani.com/unselfish-work-true-renunciation-swami-vivekananda

11. On Professor Max Müller- Swami Vivekananda
https://vivekavani.com/professor-max-muller-swami-vivekananda

12. My Master – Swami Vivekananda
https://vivekavani.com/my-master-swami-vivekananda

The Man Behind The Pen

Rohit Dey has authored several works like *Find Me A Girlfriend, I Had A Dream, Just The Touch of a Coffee Cup, and You and I—Before It's a Sunrise.* He loves to explore several genres, through both fiction and non-fiction. He has attempted diverse writings that encompass fantasy, mystery, and mythology which cater to the audience of young adults. He is currently pursuing his doctoral research in Film and Cultural Studies at Manipal University Jaipur. Apart from being an amateur writer and a keen researcher, he is a passionate fashion enthusiast and a certified fitness expert.

Printed by Libri Plureos GmbH in Hamburg, Germany